"This is the book our marketing students have been waiting for. It blends theory and practice seamlessly and makes sure that the skills needed to become successful, both on their course and in their future job, are embedded in every chapter. The writing is engaging and informative and the use of real-life case studies helps bring the subject to life. Highly recommended!"

**Dr Peter Wolstencroft, BSc (Econ), PGCE, MA, PhD, SFHEA, CMBE,**
*Deputy Director, Liverpool Business School, Liverpool John Moores University*

"*Marketing Skills in Practice* provides a comprehensive and contemporary overview of the essential marketing skills required in today's competitive business landscape – skills which take the reader beyond those specific to marketing – management, leadership, reflection. The text adeptly combines theoretical concepts with practical applications, enabling readers to bridge the gap between classroom knowledge and real-world marketing scenarios. The writing style is clear and concise, making complex marketing principles accessible and engaging for readers of all levels of expertise. The authors have masterfully curated a wealth of industry insights, case studies and real-life examples that provide a rich learning experience. This approach ensures that readers not only comprehend the fundamental concepts but also develop a keen understanding of their practical implications."

**Dr Karen Hadley, PhD, MA, LLB, PFHEA,**
*Director (Academic), Institute of Business, Industry, and Leadership,*
*University of Cumbria*

# Marketing Skills in Practice

Based around research into marketing education and marketing practice, *Marketing Skills in Practice: Developing a Successful Marketing Career* helps students embarking on their career to develop their professional identity as well as the key skills required by employers in the industry.

Divided into four core sections, the book begins with an overview of the field of marketing. Section two shows students how to relate practice to their own transferable skills, while section three gives students the opportunity to consider how they lead, develop, and manage within marketing. Section four provides students with the opportunity to reflect on their own learning and identify what knowledge and skills they have enhanced for their future careers. Fundamentally, the book identifies the key skills required in the marketing industry whilst also addressing the challenge of developing a career in leading and managing in a marketing context. Theoretical aspects are applied through real-life cases, practical examples, and a themed case study, coupled with tasks that allow students to test and apply their knowledge to a workplace scenario, all of which are adaptable for hybrid teaching methods.

Unique in its focus on employability, this text is suitable for all marketing students embarking on a career in the field, and particularly as core reading for any modules based on marketing in practice and professional development.

Online resources include PowerPoint slides for lecturers and an instructor's manual, which includes lesson plans, tasks, suggested answers, and a test bank with answers.

**Dr Linda Anne Barkas** is Senior Lecturer in business management and Programme Leader Doctorate in business administration, Faculty of Business Law and Tourism, University of Sunderland, UK.

**Dr Yvonne Dixon-Todd** is Head of the School of Business and Management, Faculty of Business Law and Tourism, University of Sunderland, UK.

# Marketing Skills in Practice

Developing a Successful Marketing Career

Dr Linda Anne Barkas and
Dr Yvonne Dixon-Todd

Routledge
Taylor & Francis Group

LONDON AND NEW YORK

Designed cover image: Egor Suvorov

First published 2024
by Routledge
4 Park Square, Milton Park, Abingdon, Oxon OX14 4RN

and by Routledge
605 Third Avenue, New York, NY 10158

*Routledge is an imprint of the Taylor & Francis Group, an informa business*

*British Library Cataloguing-in-Publication Data*
A catalogue record for this book is available from the British Library

*Library of Congress Cataloging-in-Publication Data*
Names: Barkas, Linda, author. | Dixon-Todd, Yvonne, author.
Title: Marketing skills in practice : developing a successful marketing career / Linda Barkas and Yvonne Dixon-Todd.
Description: First edition. | New York, NY : Routledge, 2024. | Includes bibliographical references and index.
Identifiers: LCCN 2023028268 (print) | LCCN 2023028269 (ebook) | ISBN 9781032429755 (hardback) | ISBN 9781032429748 (paperback) | ISBN 9781003365136 (ebook)
Subjects: LCSH: Marketing—Vocational guidance.
Classification: LCC HF5415.35 .B37 2024 (print) | LCC HF5415.35 (ebook) | DDC 658.8007—dc23/eng/20230717
LC record available at https://lccn.loc.gov/2023028268
LC ebook record available at https://lccn.loc.gov/2023028269

ISBN: 978-1-032-42975-5 (hbk)
ISBN: 978-1-032-42974-8 (pbk)
ISBN: 978-1-003-36513-6 (ebk)

DOI: 10.4324/9781003365136

Typeset in Berling
by Apex CoVantage, LLC

Access the Support Material: www.routledge.com/9781032429748

To my father, Edward John Bruce. – Dr Linda Anne Barkas

To my niece and nephew, Jessica and Sebastian Healey. – Dr Yvonne Dixon-Todd

# Contents

# Acknowledgements

The authors would like to thank the contributors to the book:

Mohammad Adwan, Okikiola Akingbo, Paul-Alan Armstrong, Jane Bell, Garry Bishop, Ian Carr, Peter Coleman, Andrew Dean, Alessandro Ferrazza, Empire Cinemas, Greggs, Paul Harm, Jessica and Sebastian Healey, Peter Henry, John Husband, Connor Moore, Olubukola Owolabi, Anish Patel, Lauren Paton, Graeme Price, Royal Jordanian Airlines, Kelly Shotton, Craig Southern, Benjamin Spence, Carol Stoker, Veronica Swindale, Totrain, Gareth Trainer, Tony Walker, Derek Watson, Ryan Williams, Kris Woods.

Thank you for the permission to the organisations and Pexels (Free Stock Photos, Royalty Free Stock Images & Copyright Free Pictures, Pexels) to include the photographs and images. Credit to the originators:

Philip Akerman, Certified Carbon Literate, CMI, Cottonbro Studio, Empire Cinemas, Alena Darmel, Dinelle De Veyra, Kindel Media, Mikail Nilov, Royal Jordanian Airlines, Alekandra Pasaric, Andrea Plasquadio, Rodnae Productions, Jose Francisco Fernandez Saura, Sora Shimzaki, University of Sunderland (Media Office).

Authors' personal appreciation to family and friends:

Many thanks to Chris and my brother Graeme for their love, support, and encouragement throughout our personal and business lives together. Love always, Linda. A special thanks to truly authentic leaders – Roger Spence and all the business colleagues I have had the pleasure of working for and with over so many years; too many more to mention, but your knowledge, skills, and guidance have stayed with me (and I still have that dictionary, Len!) Love always, Linda.
With thanks to my lovely family, David, Angus, and Chloe; my parents, Doreen and Herbie; and my sister Wendy and her family. Thank you for all your support in everything I do in life. Love to you all. Yvonne.

# Author profiles

**FIGURE FM.1** Linda Anne Barkas, PhD.

**Linda Anne Barkas** is a senior lecturer in business management at the University of Sunderland, a senior fellow of the HEA, a member of ILM, CIM, BSA, and CMI, and on the editorial board of several international journals. Linda joined the University of Sunderland after working as a freelance teacher and management consultant. She worked in administration and senior management in the public and private sectors and owned several businesses before retraining as an English as a second language teacher and travelling abroad. This led to a career change into FE for 13 years and then a move into research in HE, where she has gained over 30 years' experience of managing, teaching, supervision, and research. She is currently a member of the professional doctorate team, where she is the module leader for research methods and programme leader for the forthcoming doctorate in business administration. Linda is the director of studies and co-supervisor for a number of students researching different aspects of business and marketing management. Her research interests and publications are in teaching and learning in higher education, and she has supervised research students from different disciplines undertaking a variety of projects, from issues in health and safety, management in professions allied to health, to managing change in business environments. Previous roles have included as the interim team leader for the leadership and HRM and strategy and operations teams; programme leader for the MBA and MA international management; centre leader for three of our partners in Vietnam; and module leader for the dissertation on the MAIM programme.

**FIGURE FM.2** Yvonne Dixon-Todd, DProf.

**Yvonne Dixon-Todd** is the head of the School of Business and Management at the University of Sunderland. Yvonne is a marketer at heart and has held various marketing roles in the industry. Now working as an academic, she has been involved in marketing for over 30 years. Yvonne is a Fellow of the Chartered Institute of Marketing (FCIM), a Chartered Member in Business Management (CMBE), and a Senior Fellow of the Higher Education Academy (SFHEA). She has held the posts of an examiner, deputy chair, and member of the Learning Advisory Group with the Chartered Institute of Marketing and as the deputy chair of the Marketing

Pedagogy Special Interest Group within the Academy of Marketing. Her focus now is on leading an internationally and professionally connected business school. Her research interests are in the integration of marketing disciplines and enhancing student experience through innovative pedagogy. She is the founder of the Sunderland Marketing Hub, which provides a unique opportunity for academics, students, and practitioners to come together on all things marketing. Her research interests lie in integrated marketing, marketing communications, and pedagogy. She has published international conference papers and journal articles and works as an academic reviewer for various international conferences and journals. She is proud to lead a strong and successful team that is focused and experienced in delivering innovative teaching, undertaking research with impact, and providing a supportive and collaborative learning community.

## CHAPTER 1

# Understanding the role and scope of marketing

## SYNOPSIS AND LEARNING OUTCOMES

At the end of this chapter, successful students will be able to do the following:

1.  Compare and contrast different definitions of marketing.
2.  Explain the differing roles of marketing.
3.  Appreciate the wide scope of marketing in different organisations.

## INTRODUCTION

This chapter will encourage you to think about what marketing means to you and others, what activities it entails, and how it is undertaken. You may or may not already know some theory about marketing; however, everyone will have some experiences of marketing already. This is because marketing is all round us, every day!

## WHAT IS MARKETING?

This is a question that is asked in most degree classes and hotly debated in the professional world. There are many viewpoints, and it is important that someone studying and/ or working in any aspect of marketing understands the different definitions/viewpoints. There are similarities and differences between definitions, depending on interest, experience, and perspective, as well as organisational structures, industries, and international contexts, and so it is important to appreciate these nuances. As a starting point, let's consider basic definitions of marketing.

The *Oxford Learners Dictionary* (2023) defines *marketing* as 'the activity of presenting, advertising and selling a company's products or services in the best possible way'.

DOI: 10.4324/9781003365136-1

**FIGURE 1.3** Photo of bridge in blue.

Utilising the latest artificial intelligence (AI) technology, we will try ChatGPT to gain insight into marketing. ChatGPT (2023) was presented with the question 'What is marketing?' and the following detailed response is noted:

> Marketing is the process of identifying, anticipating, and satisfying customer needs and wants through the creation, promotion, and distribution of products or services. It involves researching and understanding target markets, developing, and positioning products and services, creating effective communication strategies, and building and maintaining relationships with customers. Marketing involves a range of activities such as market research, product development, pricing, advertising, promotion, and distribution. It also includes building and managing a brand, analysing customer feedback and data, and constantly adapting to changing market trends and consumer behaviours. Overall, the goal of marketing is to create and deliver value to customers, build long-term relationships, and ultimately drive business growth and profitability.

The authors agree with the AI chat box here! Yes, this is an excellent summary of what *marketing* is. The nuances mentioned earlier, however, are in how best to conduct all these activities and be successful – and indeed, be more successful than your competitors! And while computer technology is becoming a huge part of marketing, it is still us, humans, who are making the data informed decisions!

**FIGURE 1.4** Marketing whiteboard. Handshake over whiteboard.

Now we will consider some well-known definitions, such as that of the Chartered Institute of Marketing (CIM), based in the UK; the American Marketing Association (AMA), based in America; and the marketing guru Philip Kotler (2000).

The CIM (2023) states that *marketing* is:

> The management process responsible for identifying, anticipating and satisfying customer requirements profitably.

And the AMA (2023) states that:

> Marketing is the activity, set of institutions, and processes for creating, communicating, delivering, and exchanging offerings that have value for customers, clients, partners, and society at large.

Kotler (1994) created a definition of *marketing* that is still used today when he said that:

> Marketing is a social and managerial process by which individuals and groups obtain what they need and want through creating and exchanging products and value with other.

As you read more about marketing, you will find many more definitions abound. For example:

> If I was to define marketing, I would lean towards the CIM definition. . . . I see marketing as something that we all do, every day, without realising. Marketing is about identifying, generating, and sharing value, it can be tangible or intangible, and results in a positive (or indeed, less negative) exchange for all parties involved.
>
> (Dixon-Todd, 2019)

When thinking about marketing in an organisation, you need to consider the related activities. Activities centred on, for example, customer experience, customer services, public relations, branding, sales, and even operations may be a part of marketing. In some instances, the interactions between these departments can be very frequent and very challenging for marketers. In many organisations, marketing is often perceived as just communications or, even worse, just advertising. The digital technological developments mean that it is very difficult for organisations to manage a consistent 'voice', 'service', and 'speedy response'. Aspects of this will be considered in further chapters.

Why is it important to understand what marketing means to different people? As you will see from the definitions, the place of value of the product or service is critical. Customers and consumers are addressed differently in the marketing process. What is a *customer*? What is a *consumer*? A *customer* is someone who buys the product, and the *consumer* uses it or, in the case of food, eats it! In any case, you will see from different marketing campaigns that it is important to ensure the message of the product is presented appropriately to the customer or consumer or both. Therefore, we can start to see that in all definitions, there are key themes about knowing who your customer is, understanding what your customer wants and needs (there is a difference), targeting the right customer to enable an organisation to meet its objectives, exchanging value, and doing all this better than your competitors do. Every company markets itself – even if it does nothing, that says something to the customers and wider stakeholders!

Alongside knowing what *marketing* means, we should consider the different formats marketing can take and how its role has changed in response to actual and anticipated changes in society. Marketing is many things, but most activities fall into one of the following:

Marketing as a *function*.
Marketing as a *business philosophy*.
Marketing as a *process*.

We will now explore each of these in more detail.

## SEPARATE ROLES OF MARKETING

### Marketing as a function

The way the role of marketing is conducted varies from one organisation to another. It can have a functional or strategic approach, and it can be undertaken with an art or science-based focus; however, it usually involves management of marketing within a unit/function. Large organisations may have a centralised marketing department, while others may choose a more decentralised system. As marketing has developed to include more specialised components, some companies may choose to have niche teams or outsource their marketing activities to marketing specialists. As companies organise their marketing activities in different ways, there are many career opportunities available to you. If you consider how a product, process, or service is marketed and the many ways this is organised in a company, there are, therefore, many career opportunities here as organisations seek to build capabilities in marketing. The organisations that do marketing best are more likely to be more successful. Companies structure their marketing activities in different ways; it is up to you to research and identify these, to see if it is somewhere you would like to work.

Dr Yvonne Dixon-Todd explains what her role looked like in marketing:

> I originally worked as a marketing assistant in a subsidiary company. I looked after the full marketing mix, although there was a focus on marketing communications. The commercial activity was then centralised, and I became a marketing manager for a number of subsidiaries. Over time, this role grew significantly, cooperating with internal and external specialists.

Marketing, consists of a number of activities that include strategy, planning, budget keeping, research, communications (including sales promotion, advertising, personal selling, direct marketing, and public relations), digital, and basically doing what CIM says – identifying and satisfying a market. There are many marketing tools and techniques that help explain what this entails, which we will explore in later chapters.

Large organisations often make marketing a functional process across specialist teams and departments. Examples of the types of teams/specialists can be seen by considering the example professional bodies that influence or represent marketers:

American Marketing Association: www.ama.org
Chartered Institute of Marketing: www.cim.co.uk
Marketing Society: www.marketingsociety.com
Data and Marketing Association: www.dma.org.uk
Chartered Institute of Public Relations: www.cipr.co.uk
Institute of Advertising Practitioners: www.ipa.co.uk
Academy of Marketing: www.academyofmarketing.org

Developing a professional identity in a marketing career is further explored in Chapter 6.

Whatever the activity that is being undertaken, the aim is for there to be exchanges of value to each party. This can be, and often is, monetary, but it does not need to be – it literally can be anything (think about bartering activity/giving time or support, for instance).

## Marketing as a business philosophy

You may have heard that marketing is a business philosophy – but what does this mean? It means that there is an understanding and underpinning that identifying and satisfying customers is at the core of all activities. The focus of marketing in an organisation has increased over the past few decades and has been shown as a four-stage process by Bains and Fill (2014, p. 9) as follows:

*Stage 1. 1890s–1920s: Production.* This period is termed the 'production' stage of marketing development because as goods were limited, there was little competition.

*Stage 2. 1920s–1950s: Sales.* After the First World War, market research, advertising, and personal selling developed.

*Stage 3. 1950s–1980s: Marketing.* During this time, there was further study of what the customer wanted, and market research started in earnest.

*Stage 4. 1980s onwards: Societal marketing.*

Thus, we can see that there has been a shift through the decades, from production of goods to sales advertising and then to societal marketing. The theory of marketing as a business philosophy also links with the idea of a marketing orientation or concept. The marketing orientation/concept is the most popular approach towards marketing these days, largely because it is very difficult for a business to succeed now if they do not focus on identifying and satisfying their customers' needs and wants. You can see that through having this orientation, the focus of the company is about identifying who your customers are, what your customers want now and how you can provide this better than your competitors, and what your customers will want in the future. This is where the role of marketing research and marketing insight comes into play. Organisations need to consider how they can meet needs and wants whilst also considering wider society and the impact they have on it.

## Marketing as a process

Marketing is often seen as a process that needs to be followed. This is where there are many models and tools that relate to the 'what' and the 'how'. Whilst this book can't cover all these, there is some discussion of key marketing knowledge, and this is where you will find more discussion on what marketing strategy and marketing planning are and how these fit in the wider organisational context. As marketing has become more specialised, a number of acronyms have emerged to show how the various components are combined, and we introduce a few of them next. Starting with the marketing mix. The way the process of marketing is conducted is called the *marketing mix*. The term originated when Neil Borden taught at Harvard University in the 1950s and borrowed the 'mix' idea from cookery when he described marketing managers as people who mix ingredients to find the right 'recipe' for a product or service for customers (Borden, 1964). While the list was made up of all the critical parts of marketing, it was a long list, and it was McCarthy (1960) who combined the different aspects of the marketing mix to the more memorable 4Ps:

*Product.* The item, including packaging and how it meets customers' needs.
*Place.* The distribution of the product.

*Price*. The cost to the customer, including the profit to the seller.

*Promotion*. This includes how the different parts of the item/service are presented to the customer.

The original 4Ps mix, defined by McCarthy and popularised by Kotler (1994), as noted earlier, is a well-known 4Ps – product, promotion (marketing communications), price, and place (distribution/channels). If we are to consider the extended marketing mix, then an additional 3Ps – people, physical evidence, and process – are to be considered. There have been many iterations of the Ps; however, the 4Ps have stood the test of time. As more services, experience, and types of activities are undertaken, marketers have to consider the best way of managing integrated activities to ensure there is a consistent level of quality, service, and so on. We will consider the marketing mix further in a later chapter.

There are other parts of the process. We will now start to examine the importance of the company's objectives and position, and in subsequent chapters, we will look more closely at the positioning of the product through segmentation, targeting and positioning, the concept of positioning, and the principles of perceptual mapping.

## THE MAIN TYPES OF POSITIONING STRATEGIES

*Objectives positioning strategy*. This is critical because it sets a clear direction, providing a focus in a timeline, and ensures the communication of values and scope of activities for all involved.

*Positioning strategy through a strategic business unit (SBU)*. Very large businesses often have a specialist unit that is responsible for the creation of business objectives, production, finance, and marketing.

*First-level positioning*. This is the mission and overall direction of the company.

*Communications positioning strategies*. Communications strategies or campaign objectives are the how/what and in what way the goal of the brand is positioned. Different brands have a variety of goals. For example, the goal of the owners of historical buildings may be to attract more tourists, who will pay a fee to visit the preserved buildings of historic interest. The marketing professionals responsible for the historical buildings may endeavour to encourage repeat visits by adding in different types of attractions each year.

Marketing managers must consider sales turnover. For example, the promotion of certain food in televised food programmes may impact on the types of goods shoppers then buy. *Defining Advertising Goals for Measured Advertising Results* (DAGMAR, Colley (1961), cited in Fill and Turnbull, 2019), proposed a communication model on awareness, comprehension, conviction, and action. As in the example noted earlier of the televised food programme, viewers' awareness is raised, and they may then have the conviction to find the food and take action to purchase it. Marketing teams working on these campaign objectives must therefore examine how customers can be aware of the product and by what means. Once awareness is created, the target audience must be identified. The specialist aspects must also be evaluated, and of course, the hierarchy of campaign goals is utilised here. Starting with the immediate (awareness), behaviour (loyalty/impact), and business (sales, price sensitivity). Overall, the chosen positioning strategy that is engaged must be *SMART*, that is, specific, measurable, achievable, realistic, and targeted and timed.

As can be seen, marketing contains both art and science aspects. It requires significant research and information gathering and processing to ensure an organisation fully understand its market and creativity is needed to fully reach the market. Digital marketing and the increase in data-driven decisions have started to see the art and science elements merge more closely together.

Throughout all the aforementioned activities, marketers need to consider what the value is and what the full exchange involves. Once the value has been identified, it is then about how this can be delivered better than competitors. You may have heard of terms here such as 'unique selling point' (USP), customer value, and relationship marketing. All these activities would be expected within an organisation following the marketing process.

So far, we have introduced marketing definitions and the role of marketing. We also want to share with you our findings from primary research with practitioners and academics. Within the following chapters we will introduce you to the findings of our research into integrated marketing communications, which was part of a doctoral journey. The research considered perspectives and practices of integrated marketing communications (IMC), a key part of marketing, with academic, students, and practitioners, which we think you will find useful. We hope you enjoy reading about our insights included in relevant chapters and that it helps you start thinking about how you might best develop a career in leading and managing marketing in an environment with many challenges. So thinking about marketing and the role of marketing in different organisations, some of the issues that need to be considered are:

Theory versus practice
Ownership and merging of disciplines
Key challenges
Skills and knowledge needed
What the future might hold

A brief oversight of the research findings is provided next.

## Theory versus practice

Academics expect more theory than practice, which is not really a surprise! Students see integrated marketing communications (IMC) as something to be done, as do practitioners (Dixon-Todd and Hall, 2018). Most practitioners recognise the need for education, though, to ensure employees know what is working/not working and, importantly, why this is/is not the case. Practitioners are designing and delivering IMC even if they don't call it IMC. Basically, you need to know the theory behind various marketing activities to ensure that you know what to do and, if something is not working, the reasons for this and what can be done about it. Knowing the best practice and sharing ideas help marketers learn.

## Ownership and merging of disciplines

Academics recognise that IMC is pulling together marketing disciplines as they cross over particularly at the tactical level. They do, however, recognise that IMC is much more than this, when taking the strategic approach; but this makes it much more difficult. Practitioners are openly less concerned about the fluidity of disciplines and are encroaching upon previously distinct activities. There is acknowledgement that the industry is changing, and agencies and individuals are expected to change with it.

## Challenges

This research has identified that key challenges for IMC centre on the interdisciplinary nature of IMC, lack of digital knowledge, and integrating digital into IMC and resources. Students have challenges about studying, per se, which include working with others, time commitments, reading, and relating theory to practice. They also have some challenges in identifying the tactical and the strategic nature of IMC, how IMC differs to marketing communications, and observing IMC in practice. Things that impact practitioners include developments in technology and digital, the speed of change in the industry, and keeping skills and knowledge up to date.

## Skills and knowledge needed

Key issues in skills and knowledge from academic participants centred on the amount of theory to include and how best to show theory in practice, how to integrate key subjects in the curricula, how to collaborate with other disciplines, and how to offer experiential learning and employability opportunities.

The feedback from the practitioners is extensive and demonstrates the breadth of skills required by someone to successfully progress in a career in marketing. This supports the various views put forward in the academic and practitioner literature; for instance, Spector (2015) listed ten integrated marketing communications activities that cross over digital, content marketing, PR, management, creativity, analytics, coordination, and the ability to see the bigger picture. There is a need to have an all-rounder who appreciates the benefits of the individual disciplines but who is also able to manage tactical and strategic IMC and cope with change which crosses all aspects of the developments in digital technology.

Practitioners stated that organisations are attempting to practice integrated marketing communications (IMC), even if they call it something different – such as orchestrated or consistent marketing – and see it is a natural way of working. They are more accepting of the fluidity and fluxing nature of IMC. They do, however, have significant problems when attempting to practice IMC both at the tactical and strategic level – for instance, the crossover and merging of traditional discipline areas, non-traditional job roles, and functions; the speed and growth of digital technology; the ability to attract and develop staff with traditional and new media skills and those with generalist IMC skills.

There also continues to be issues with how professional bodies recognise and accept IMC whilst protecting their own identities. When drawing all this together, and in summary, it is evident that there are some significant differences between practitioners and academia when considering perspectives and practices of IMC and IMC education. It is important that academia recognises and responds to these differences when developing and enhancing IMC programmes. Areas for focus centre on the following themes: (1) terminology, (2) theory and/or practitioner discourse, (3) levelness, (4) professional identity and ownership, and (5) skills gaps.

We will provide further insight into our research findings later in the book.

The following case studies provide examples of how our academic and practitioner experts started their careers, what they do now, and how they define *marketing*.

# CASE STUDIES

## Careers in marketing

### CASE STUDY 1.1

*Mr Benjamin Spence*

My current job title is as academic tutor, and I am also working towards a PhD in marketing. Within the University of Sunderland, I have the privilege of being part of the marketing and digital academic team, which allows me to teach on both undergraduate and postgraduate marketing modules. These have included digital marketing, marketing strategy, and markets and marketing in a digital world. I have also had the opportunity to be involved with our on-campus marketing agency, which has involved coaching students as they prepare to pitch to live clients. This has included several local SME case studies to larger corporations such as Greggs, as part of the Greggs Marketing Challenge. When the agency has hosted events such as the 'Marketing Matters' series (contemporary discussions from a panel of practitioner and academics), I have led the branding, marketing collateral, and project management of the technical 'behind the scenes' aspects to ensure the events run smoothly.

**FIGURE 1.5** Ben Spence.

In terms of research, my PhD is focused on transformational marketing, particularly in terms of inclusive masculinity and the UK football environment. This is a timely topic centred on diversity and inclusion within an environment often perceived as hypermasculine and heteronormative. My thesis explores the role of marketing in culturally evolving societal spaces, mindful of the current climate and the values and attributes held by the Generation Z and the future consumers from the Generation Alpha cohort.

I define *marketing* as the heartbeat of any business; you can have the best product or service in the world, but if people (in particular, your target market) are not aware of it, then the business will be unsustainable. Marketing allows the opportunity to think creatively on attracting the target market to the business, to resonate your brand cognitively within the mass market, and to capture that all-important market share. The marketing stream, be that of revenue generation or branding, is what creates the opportunity for the business to be sustainable and grow accordingly.

## CASE STUDY 1.2

### Dr Andrew Kristoffer Dean

I am currently employed as an associate head of marketing and digital in Sunderland University's Business School. This post is a mix of team leadership, management, research, and engaging with external organisations.

I have had an unusual career, starting out in the natural sciences, where I worked in pharmaceuticals, biotechnology, and nanotechnology; in the laboratory; and in senior management. While I enjoyed this work, I retrained in marketing and cognitive science and am now more interested in understanding fundamental scientific processes related to marketing management and communication. Having said this, as life is an ongoing process of personal reinvention, I am refocusing part of my goals towards exploring the genetic basis of our decision making.

**FIGURE 1.6** Dr Andrew Kristoffer Dean.

I define *marketing* as a fundamental process of life. Explicitly, marketing is a communicative act between individuals or species that influences value creation/destruction. Modes of communication include vocalisations, body language, chemical interactions, and just being in the world. There is much to be learnt from 'peacocking'.

## CASE STUDY 1.3

*Veronica Swindale*

Veronica Swindale, Managing Director of Nesma, an accredited study centre for Chartered Institute of Marketing and Chartered Institute of Public Relations qualifications and in-house training in marketing, communications, and digital, describes her role as follows:

FIGURE 1.7 Veronica Swindale.

My role is to steer the business to ensure that our courses provision meets the needs of our clients and that we have the right team and resources in place to deliver that. Historically, we prided ourselves on delivering face-to-face teaching in a very informal and supportive educational environment, but when Covid arrived, we consulted with all our tutors and our clients and their employees to create a similarly supportive online but interactive experience.

Fortunately, everyone was happy to embrace the online learning environment. This has afforded us the opportunity to grow our markets throughout the UK, and in 2023, we are working in more than 20 different countries across the globe. If I hadn't seen people being held at gunpoint in Italy on

# nesma

BUILDING MARKETING KNOW-HOW

FIGURE 1.8 Logo of Nesma.

the evening news when movement was restricted in the name of Covid protection, we may not have acted for a few weeks, and complacency wouldn't have led to the success we are now experiencing today.

We are just entering a further new growth phase where we are pursuing wider opportunities and restructuring and recruiting to optimise these opportunities. We are fortunate to have extremely well-qualified and experienced tutors who are all practitioners and/or academics who do a brilliant job in inspiring our students, and this team continues to grow.

I first moved to Newcastle when I was 24 and took up a role with a marine consultancy company that worked around the world. Whilst at this company, I undertook an RSA teaching diploma, then a postgraduate diploma in management studies, and the CIM postgraduate diploma in marketing. I also studied for the Institute of Linguists diploma in French and GCSE Spanish to assist with some of the contracts we had secured in Cherbourg, Algeria, and Mexico.

This was followed by a career portfolio of marketing consultancy, training, and lecturing. It also led me to working as a sales and marketing manager for a drug manufacturer owned by an American company larger than Microsoft at that time. Not many people know that I used to be a drug dealer!

I also embarked upon an Open University MBA, and my latest qualification is a Certificate in Carbon Literacy. I was one of the world's first chartered marketers, an achievement celebrated with 1,000 fellow chartered marketers at the Royal Festival Hall in London. All these qualifications have served me very well, and I am convinced I use my management learning almost on a daily basis. I strongly believe that everyone should continue to learn throughout their lives. At no point do we know it all, as things around us are changing so dramatically all the time, and it is important to understand all the functions and perspectives of any organisation we work in.

I love working with our clients and, across the years, have taught thousands from the very first principles of marketing through to the master's programmes, where you can see real-life scenarios being tackled strategically and learners taking their research back into the workplace. Assignment topics range from addressing the lack of diversity or digitalisation in an organisation's structure or way of working through to some technological solutions to assist businesses to support their customers better, whether that be a smart piece of kit to ship abnormal loads around the world or simply a more efficient CRM system. We work with employees from many of the big brands, significant departments from local and central government, the NHS, SMEs, and the third sector.

I love to hear our own student stories to learn how doing our courses has helped them evolve not only their marketing skills but their personal skills too. The most common phrase we hear at master's level is, 'I'm doing this for me'; at all levels it's about 'the confidence this learning has given [someone] to make the right decisions'.

Marketing is about providing solutions for things people need in a way that you become their first choice every time and that they recommend you voluntarily to family and friends and via social media to the world as a whole. The challenge comes in delivering consistently a high level of service and being able to expand comfortably into bigger shoes.

Key drivers for good marketing strategies currently are the capability to gather insightful data, upon which you can take effective marketing decisions, and the proactive use of artificial intelligence to automate your repetitive transactions yet enable you still to have a 'personal' relationship with each of your clients or service users. At the time of writing, net zero operations, akin to corporate social responsibility, or environmental social governance, are key to business thinking.

Planning is key, but unless you have the whole organisation on board and engaged in the new plan, you risk not succeeding.

Young marketers starting out should aim to get as much experience as possible, ideally whilst still at school or university. Please volunteer or get a part-time job. Serving in a shop or café will give you wonderful insights into how many ways people think differently about, say, what makes a good coffee in their eyes to how friendly or unfriendly they are when you present the bill. The more you can understand how people think and behave, the more you can adapt your marketing strategy to meet their needs better and more often than your competitors do.

I look forward to seeing how Nesma grows in the next five years and wonder what technological and currently unknown drivers we will have embraced on that journey!

## CASE STUDY 1.4

*Kris Woods*

**FIGURE 1.9** Certified Carbon Literate.

I am a chartered marketer and fellow of the Chartered Institute of Marketing, with years of industry experience within retail in-house marketing, local advertising agencies, and the regional press. I have worked at the board level and in a wide range of areas, including corporate communications, strategic marketing planning, promotions, public relations, and event management, before entering the world of academia in 2014.

**FIGURE 1.10** CIM membership badge

Whilst I currently work as an academic tutor with the University of Sunderland Business School, delivering a range of marketing and management learning to undergraduate and postgraduate students, my career in marketing started awhile back, working as a copywriter (content creator) for House of Frazer's Binns brand, a group of 17 department stores located across northern England and southern Scotland.

Here, I had the privilege of working for Joan McDonald, a highly respected doyen of the North-East advertising industry and a great mentor. Long before Michael Porter had established his expertise in the field, she taught me all about marketing, including the importance of creating a mental picture of your target customer every time you write and ensuring you speak directly to them to generate the appropriate response; and I am glad to say that we, marketers, are still using this approach today, evidenced in the use of formalised customer personas and the ongoing drive to ensure the right message is seen by the right person, in the right media, and at the right time.

However, whilst some principles still hold strong, the world of marketing is constantly changing; indeed, it has changed significantly since my early days, which is why I am a staunch advocate of continuous professional development (CPD) and ongoing learning. It is what enables me to remain relevant in an increasingly digital world. An integral element of my own CPD was the achievement of the CIM professional diploma in marketing, an applied learning programme which required the assimilation of my practical skills and experience with the academic tools and models of marketing. As a result, I have a multifaceted approach to marketing, which has helped me deliver successful marketing programmes in industry and, more recently, in the classroom.

The key themes of my teaching approach are to create a lively environment which is enjoyable for the students and encourages discussion, debate, and critical thinking. In my teaching and learning delivery, my preference is to encourage my students to undertake active listening. For example, undertaking analysis of case study material and using real-life situations to challenge critical thinking. I believe that students who actively participate in their learning experience, rather than being passive in the learning process, develop better levels of critical thinking, and this, in turn, further stimulates their cognitive processes and adds to their learning experience. In addition, I strongly believe that a theoretical knowledge of marketing combined with a practical application is the best approach, as this allows students to contextualise their learning; it also better prepares them for the rigours of the workplace too. This is the methodology I adopt when mentoring the university's team for the Greggs marketing. Here, I prepare the student team for an external competition and liaise with Greggs and other competing universities, to ensure the preparation and delivery of this external event runs seamlessly. This role includes coaching students to create, prepare, and present work to a professional industry standard.

Additionally, I provide mentor support to students in the university's master's programme to help them achieve the best possible outcomes for their degree programme, and it is here they can really investigate their chosen career path in marketing. If they choose to research the industry or sector where they want to work, they have a good grounding and understanding to include in their personal profile or on their CV.

I am currently developing my research voice through a professional doctorate, building on my MBA research into the relevance of, and academic and practical outcomes generated from, delivery of germane Carbon Literacy training to staff and students within the Faculty of Business, Law, and Tourism at the University of Sunderland. We live in a climate emergency, and countries, companies, and consumers alike are increasingly recognising the need to deliver against the UN Sustainable Development Goals; added to this, there is a shift happening as consumers are made aware of issues around climate change and sustainability and are increasingly basing their purchasing decisions on this knowledge. This impacts all elements of the marketing mix, which now needs to be viewed through the lens of sustainability.

**Jessica Healey, aged 10, a potential future marketer**

And here's a little poem for you all to consider.

Think of a product to start to construct for your market,

Develop and make your merchandise,

Make sure it's something to catch people's eyes,

What could it be?

Your item one or two, it's up to you,

Make your dream come true.

The following case study is an example of a live marketing student and business project.

## CASE STUDY 1.5

*Dr Graeme Price*

**Students' marketing project for Empire Cinemas**

As part of the understanding markets and marketing module at the University of Sunderland, students undertook a visit to Empire Cinemas, Sunderland. The assessment for the module was based upon the organisation, and students were required to investigate and analyse the cinema's

**FIGURE 1.11** Empire Cinemas arena.

marketing strategy, incorporating customer engagement approaches, competitor analysis, and suggesting recommendations to move the business forward.

As such, the visit allowed students to see the operational elements of the cinema, hear about marketing strategies from senior marketing managers, and undertake a Q&A to gain first-hand primary research for their assignment.

This approach to linking assessment and 'real-life' business allowed for the module leader to demonstrate theoretical knowledge to practical examples. Reflections from students were also very positive, who acknowledged that their learning was enhanced through this teaching method.

The following case study offers an insight into how an airline markets its services.

## CASE STUDY 1.6

*Mohammad Adwan*

### Royal Jordanian Airline

#### Airline overview

His Majesty King Hussein of Jordan issued a royal decree to establish a national airline in 1963. His words left a lasting impression; His Majesty wanted our national airline to be the ambassador of goodwill and the conduit through which we exchange culture, civilisation, trade, technology, friendship, and a

**FIGURE 1.12** Royal Jordanian Airline logo.

deeper understanding with the rest of the world. Alia (later renamed Royal Jordanian) began its operations in response to His Majesty King Hussein's vision. Royal Jordanian has long served as Jordan's national airline. Today, under the invaluable direction and directives of His Majesty King Abdullah II, the airline fulfils its mission by continuously modernising and enhancing its services, renewing its fleet, and expanding its route network and operations.

Royal Jordanian operates its flights at Queen Alia International Airport (QAIA). The airline's headquarters are located in the centre of Amman, the capital. Its contemporary fleet services 45 destinations across four continents. The airline owns Royal Wings, a Royal Jordanian subsidiary corporation specialising in the charter business and operating out of Amman Civil Airport in Marka. It also owns Tikram, the exclusive meet-and-greet service provider at QAIA, and Royal Tours, which helps RJ market its flights to tourist attractions worldwide (Royal Jordanian Annual Report, 2021). The airline was honoured to be invited by the prestigious Oneworld airline alliance to join its elite membership, which includes American Airlines, British Airways, Iberia, Cathay Pacific, Japan Airlines, and many others. Thus, RJ is the first Arab and regional airline to join any of the three global airline alliances (Oneworld, SkyTeam, and Star Alliance) and the first airline to join Oneworld in the past five years. The airline became an official member of Oneworld on April 1, 2007, after fulfilling all technical and technological requirements. Royal Jordanian has marketing alliances with several international airlines through code-sharing, including American Airlines, British Airways, US Airways, Iberia, Malev Hungarian Airlines, Tarom, Gulf Air, Syrian Arab Airlines, and Yemen Airways.

Royal Jordanian Airlines has a reputation for excellence that is enviable. The services provided to all its passengers guarantee that each flight is a singular experience. There are 3,209 employees in the Royal Jordanian family. Its employees in Amman, Queen Alia International Airport, and 58 stations across four continents operate a fleet of 24 modern aircraft (Royal Jordanian Annual Report, 2021). Now celebrating its 60th anniversary, it is a progressive organisation that is anxious to modernise its operations by improving its services. The company invests significantly in its human resources, offering incentives, training, and satisfactory retirement and compensation packages.

### Marketing journey at Royal Jordanian (RJ) Airlines

Marketing in the aviation industry is highly specialised and is conducted by a highly talented, innovative, and creative marketing team; the most recent marketing campaign, A World of Stories, focuses on providing passengers with the best possible experience and being honoured to be a part of their stories. From the instant they book their tickets until their destination, providing passengers with the most luxurious travel experiences possible (RJ Marketing Journey, 2023). During the pandemic, digital adoption became a requirement for any growing business. As a result, RJ's IT department extended the adoption of the Microsoft Customer Relationship Management platform to other business units in the sales, marketing, and airport services departments to streamline and automate administrative processes, facilitate more personalised marketing campaigns, and achieve more effective marketing activities.

In addition, RJ has entered into commercial agreements with several international airlines to operate on a code-share basis. RJ acts as the marketing carrier and places its code on flights operated by other airlines. These code-share agreements aim to expand the airline's network and reach destinations where RJ does not operate directly. This includes nonstop flights from Amman to Abu Dhabi, Bucharest, Bahrain, Beirut, Casablanca, Doha, Istanbul, Muscat, and Rome that service RJ's passengers (RJ Annual Report, 2021).

### Marketing strategy and revenue management

The objective of revenue management is relatively straightforward: to maximise revenue through a combination of pricing differentiation and inventory control, keeping in mind factors such as the demand – which varies by time of day, day of the week, season, and business cycle – and the ticket price – which varies by class of service (first, business, premium economy, or economy), the time of purchase, the booking channel (online, call centre, or through a travel agent), and the date of travel – when setting up a marketing strategy, such factors need to be considered. This relationship relates to Kotler's (2000) definition of marketing as 'meeting needs profitably', in which marketing is concerned with identifying and satisfying human and social needs.

From a marketing standpoint, it is advantageous to divide the market demand into two segments: the trade, which includes airlines that purchase airport facilities directly, and the general public or travellers, who utilise airport products. Most airports concur that both airlines and passengers are essential consumers. Consequently, and after taking into account the factors affecting the choice of airports from passengers' perspectives – for example, destinations of flights, image and reliability of airline, and range and quality of shops, F&B, and other commercial activities – and from airlines' perspectives – for example, catchment area and potential demand, slot availability, and marketing availability – the marketing mix for services identifies the characteristics of a service. It consists of the traditional 4Ps of the product marketing mix (product, promotion, price, and place), plus the 3Ps applied to services (processes, physical evidence, and people).

## TASKS FOR THIS CHAPTER

So what do you think *marketing* is?

### Task 1.1

Create your own definition of *marketing*.

### Task 1.2

Go back to your own definition of *marketing*. How does it compare to the preceding definitions? Note the similarities – or 'golden threads' – of marketing. Now think about all the marketing terms and words you have read.

### Task 1.3

Throughout the book, we explore how a fictitious vegetarian shop and café chain can market itself and develop. As you consider the synergies and differences of definitions, meanings, and approaches taken in different organisations and industries, consider the importance of the name of the product or organisation.

Imagine you are a member of the management team of a chain of vegetarian shops and cafés and believe that the store needs a fresh approach, and this will start with a new name. Explore the names of similar vegetarian shops that also combine a vegetarian café;

try to think of a new name that has already not been taken! Thinking of a name for your product (that has already not been used) is a lot harder than you would think!

Suggested responses are in Chapter 10.

## SUMMARY OF CHAPTER 1

In Chapter 1, we have considered some different definitions of *marketing*. We have considered those from the CIM, the AMA, Kotler, and even ChatGPT! Real practitioners have also provided their insights into marketing. Through reading and comparing these, you will have identified that there are, of course, differences, but there are also many similarities. It can be seen that marketing is something that is undertaken by individuals and organisations. Marketing can be a process, an activity, a department/function, a philosophy, and something that an individual or organisation can do. We have introduced you to some of the tools and techniques of marketing practiced in different organisations. Our next chapter considers the trends in marketing.

## REFERENCES

AMA. (2023) *What Is Marketing*. Available from: What is Marketing? – The Definition of Marketing – AMA (Accessed 22 April 2023).

Bains, C. and Fill, C. (2014) *Marketing*. 3rd Edition. Oxford: Oxford University Press.

Borden, N.H. (1964) The concept of the marketing mix. *Journal of Advertising Research*, 4, 2–7.

ChatGPT. (2023) Available from: Introducing ChatGPT (openai.com) (Accessed 22 April 2023).

CIM. (2015) *A Brief Summary of Marketing and How It Works*. CIM. Available from: 7ps. pdf (cim.co.uk) (Accessed 20 February 2023).

CIM. (2023) *What Is Marketing*. Available from: 7ps.pdf (cim.co.uk) (Accessed 22 April 2023).

Dixon-Todd, Y. (2019) *Enhancing the Teaching of Marketing in Higher Education: An Integrated Marketing Communications Perspective*. Professional Doctorate. University of Sunderland. Unpublished.

Dixon-Todd, Y. and Hall, L. (2018) The state of integrated marketing communications education: Insights from industry – but do we all agree? Academy of Marketing Conference Proceedings.

Fill, C. and Turnbull, S. (2019) *Marketing Communications*. Harlow: Pearson.

Kotler, P. (1994) *Marketing Management, Analysis, Planning, Implementation and Control*. 8th Edition. New Jersey: Prentice Hall.

Kotler, P. (2000) *Marketing Management. The Millennium Edition*. New Jersey: Prentice Hall.

Marketing. (2023) Marketing noun – Definition, pictures, pronunciation, and usage notes. Oxford Advanced Learner's Dictionary at OxfordLearnersDictionaries.com (Accessed 20 February 2023).

*Marketing Definition: Marketing Definition Summary.* (openai.com) (Accessed 20 February 2023).

McCarthy, E.J. (1960) *Basic Marketing.* Homewood, IL: Irwin.

RJ Marketing Journey. (2023) *Marketing Journey – Royal Jordanian.* Royal Jordanian Airlines. Available from: www.rj.com/en/meet-rj/our-media-center/marketing-journey (Accessed 28 April 2023).

Royal Jordanian Annual Report. (2021) *Annual Report Financial Statement – Royal Jordanian.* Royal Jordanian. Available from: www.rj.com/en/meet-rj/investors-relations/annual-report-financial-statement (Accessed 28 April 2023).

Spector, R. (2015) *10 Sample Job Duties That an IMC Professional May Have on Their Resume.* Public Relations Tactics, Public Relations Society of America, April 2015 Edition.

## RECOMMENDED FURTHER READING

CIM. (2015) A brief summary of marketing and how it works. CIM, 7ps.pdf (cim.co.uk) (Accessed 20 February 2023).

*Authors' comments: This publication by CIM provides a very good overview of marketing.*

Kotler, P. (2000) *Marketing Management. The Millennium Edition.* New Jersey: Prentice Hall.

*Authors' comments: Kotler has published his market research extensively and this book introduces the reader to key issues in marketing management.*

## CHAPTER 2

# Trends in marketing

## It is not all digital!

---

### SYNOPSIS AND LEARNING OUTCOMES

At the end of this chapter, successful students will be able to do the following:

1. Identify the current trends in the subject of marketing.
2. Explain the current trends in the marketing profession.
3. Evaluate the implications of current trends on marketers.

---

## INTRODUCTION

Marketing is changing as it adapts to challenges in the internal and external environment. This chapter will begin to explore some of the main changes impacting on marketing and those working in marketing, and the implications both present for marketers. Responding to these challenges means that the management of a company must design business and marketing strategies that are operationally feasible in both macroenvironmental and microenvironmental terms. In order to do this, it is critical that the management secure and respond to accurate data that will show the demographic, economic, and natural environment. From your previous studies and your working experience, you may be familiar with the term PESTLE (also, sometimes written as PESTEL), which encompasses the process of the acquisition of knowledge intelligence in terms of data collection. A reminder of the meaning of the term PESTLE is that it is an analysis of information on the key factors that impact on a company's business from the political, economic, sociological, technological, legal, and environmental external environments. Before a company can structure its microenvironmental strategies, it must fully understand the status of the current external market. We will outline each aspect of the external PESTLE and then explore the current trends in response to these challenges (Whittington et al., 2020).

DOI: 10.4324/9781003365136-2

# AN OUTLINE OF THE EXTERNAL FACTORS: A PESTLE ANALYSIS

## Political

Some factors from PESTLE may be more important to some businesses than others; however, it is critical that a company be aware of the political context in whichever country they are operating. The political factors include government controls over the economy or industry, legislation, and economic policies. These are important because the government's legislation impacts on trade tariffs, taxation, and fiscal policies. Non-governmental organisations are also included, such as the interactions between governments, regulators, charities, the media, lobbyists, public relations firms, and campaign activists. Once information of the political context is appreciated, a company would then proceed with a strategy to minimise risk. This would be undertaken through a SWOT analysis. SWOT stands for *strengths*, *weaknesses*, *opportunities*, and *threats* (SWOT is discussed in Chapter 3 and subsequent chapters). For example, since Britain left the European Union, extensive discussions and negotiations have been ongoing in how governments can legislate business transactions within and across Europe and trade across continents (Gov.UK, 2023).

## Economic

The economic environment includes all the factors that impact on supply and demand. The study of economics involves research into the complex variables that impact on the wealth of a country, such as production, distribution, and consumption of goods and services. Inflation and growth rate influence the gross domestic product. The gross domestic product (GDP) is an evaluation of the monetary status of a country's market of goods and services. The GDP is linked to the foreign exchange markets (where prices are determined as currencies are bought and sold). A company must be aware of the issues presented in the GDP when trading across countries, as a drop in the exchange rate can mean a huge financial loss to them. The GDP per capita is a combination of the goods and services in a nation and is a useful measure of the wealth between countries. The employment patterns and discretionary spending of people are thus impacted by the economic status of the environment. In April 2023, the consumer price inflation rate in the United Kingdom was 10.1%. The cost of food, housing, and utilities remained high, and this impacts on all levels of the supply chain, resulting in both companies and people having less income. Monetary policy in the UK and USA is to try to reduce inflation to encourage economic growth (Trading Economics, 2023).

## Sociological/socio-cultural

The social-cultural factors of the macroenvironmental include demographic trends, social and cultural values, attitudes and beliefs, lifestyles, and skills. A study of how all these factors interact is a key role of marketers and is explored throughout the book. Company managers and marketing teams study these interactions before formulating business strategies and marketing plans (Cole and Kelly, 2015; Trading Economics, 2023).

## Technological

Advancements in advanced and new technologies impact on all aspects of businesses, changing practices for some and providing opportunities for others. In marketing, for example, the advancements on the Internet, artificial technologies, analytics, digital technologies, mobile phones, and YouTube have impacted on the diverse channels of promotion of goods and services (Percy, 2023; CIM, 2023).

## Legal

The legal environment crosses every aspect of business, from start-up operations to global transactions. Governments develop public policy to guide commerce and business legislation. An aspect of which is the importance of ensuring safety for companies and the public. As companies open up their business internationally and/or globally, they must comply with legislation and international law. Advertising standards differ across the world, but in some countries, such as the UK, advertising is self-regulated by the Advertising Standards Agency (ASA) (2023).

## Environmental (ecological)

The natural environment is the complex relationship between natural resources and society's interaction with it. The current challenges facing business and society today are the impact of the issues emerging from pollution, global warming, safe waste disposal, sustainability, an overpopulation, and alternative energy sources rather than fossil fuels (Boyd for the Environment Agency, 2023).

To have a successful business and remain competitive, the senior management of companies will, therefore, ensure there is a current research and analysis strategy against a PESTEL framework. This analysis will then help examine current trends in marketing.

## THE CURRENT TRENDS IN THE SUBJECT OF MARKETING

The implementation of a company's microenvironmental strategies is part of the roles of managers and marketing teams and is fully examined in Chapter 3. Research into marketing, however, is a critical part of strategic forecasting for any business. Hague et al. (2016, p. 1) foresaw the impact of globalisation and digital technologies on present-day marketing when they said that '[t]he two biggest impacts on the market research world in the last few years have been the continued move towards globalization and the digital revolution'.

While the rapid development of the Internet undoubtedly opened up globalisation, large organisations started to develop in the latter part of the twentieth century. *Globalisation* refers to the growth of international markets across the world. It brings with it both opportunities and challenges. These large organisations are often termed multinational enterprises (MNEs) and may have headquarters in one country and branches in many others. Their marketing strategies are variable, with some MNEs having a global brand,

**FIGURE 2.13** Image of digital marketing.

such as Apple or Coca-Cola, whereas other companies position their products to meet local tastes (Percy, 2023).

The American Marketing Association (2023) identifies seven key challenges for marketing today:

1. Effectively target high-value sources of growth.
2. The role of marketing in the firm and the C-suite.
3. The digital transformation of the modern organisation.
4. Generating and using insight to shape marketing practice.
5. Dealing with an omnichannel world.
6. Competing in dynamic, global markets.
7. Balancing incremental and radical innovation.

Each challenge for marketing, however, also relies on the fundamental principles of marketing still being undertaken effectively. As predicted by AMA (2023), companies marketing today must therefore meet the seven challenges, as follows:

## Effectively target high-value sources of growth

Companies have to be able to segment, target, and position their offerings to maximise value. Traditionally known as segmentation, this is now also called 'demand landscape mapping' (American Marketing Association, 2023). To be able to undertake segmentation, targeting, and positioning, an organisation has to complete significant market research and ensure that they understand the needs and wants of the target market and are able to reach this target and maintain contact with this target. With analytics, consumer surveillance, and AI-driven AdTech, this process will become increasingly data-driven, with content assessed for effectiveness seamlessly and niche markets increasingly targeted (CIM, 2023).

## The role of marketing in the firm and in the C-suite

The C-suite (senior executives) are key in ensuring that marketing is established within the organisation, with marketing a core business function in the majority of sectors. Branding is a challenge particularly across multiple platforms and a potentially wide range of customers, with clear integrated marketing communication strategies needed to ensure growth. As discussed in Chapter 1, there are a variety of approaches to the location of marketing. Some organisations take a functional approach, whereby others are more strategic. Marketing can also be a centralised or decentralised department. Other organisations take an 'in-house' approach to marketing, while different companies may choose to outsource their marketing. There are many career opportunities here as organisations seek to build capabilities in marketing, and those that do it best are more likely to be more successful.

## The digital transformation of the modern organisation

Technological changes and the digital transformation have impacted significantly on marketing activity. This transformation impacts the way organisations work and interact with their markets. Media is more fragmented, and there is an increasing number of new media channels. For example, marketers must work with technologies between email/web/text/applications that have emerged. Over the past 20 years, the expansion of the Internet has been significant, with the burgeoning digital technology and the development of big data managed through data management platforms (DMPs). This term is used to describe the huge volumes of structured and unstructured data created every day (Whittington et al., 2020). *Big data* has been defined as 'high volume, velocity and variety information assets that demand cost-effective, innovative forms of information processing for enhanced insight and decision making' (Sicular, 2013, quoted in Fill and Turnbull, 2019, p. 36).

Customers and wider stakeholder groups now use computers, notebooks, laptops, mobile phones, and watches to access content. As a result, marketing departments have to be able to create compelling communications that work across all these variable platforms. This technology is continuing to develop, and so organisations such as Smart Insights (2023) have emerged to help companies with the transition to utilising digital technologies to the full. Digital marketing experts such as Smart Insights provide a service to business in what they term is a *RACE* review to help companies manoeuvre their business strategy through the complexity of digital channels. In this digital business, RACE stands for *reach, act, convert,* and *engage* (Smart Insights, 2023).

## Generating and using insight to shape marketing practice

As noted earlier, big data and constant digital engagement with consumers require integration between functions and departments seeking to maximise the value of gathered data to return value better than competitors to gain competitive advantage. This integration results in greater understanding both of consumers and of the marketing processes themselves, offering the potential to feed into continual process improvement.

## Dealing with an omnichannel world

'Omnichannel' marketing considers how social, mobile, Internet multi-channel markets and bricks and mortar can all be integrated together to target and satisfy identified markets. Orazi et al. (2017, p. 552), stated: 'Rapid evolution of digital media and the ensuing large volume of information produced have drastically changed the frequency and nature of contact points.' This has continued to the present day. Google knows what people are searching for, Facebook knows what people are interested in and whom they are connected to, and Amazon knows specifically what/frequency of products people purchase – consumer purchase data (Fill and Turnbull, 2019, p. 51). The growth of mobile technology, such as smartphones, has meant potential customers may be viewing products of interest and so 'always on', and this means the roaming capability provides extensive opportunities for marketing campaigns. Consolidation and convergence technology has therefore forced media channels together, providing extensive opportunities for advertisers. For example, Virgin and BT offer phone, broadband, and TV service packages (Kotler and Armstrong, 2020).

The combination of channels has led to the introduction of personal branding and 'influencers'. People are termed 'influencers' if they can earn an income and increase sales from personal promotion of a product or service through their personal Facebook, You-Tube, or webpage. The original influencer is often thought to be Michelle Phan, a Vietnamese American who started promoting beauty products in 2006, and her company Ipsy become a successful multi-million personal brand (Quesenberry and Coolsen, 2023). This method of personal promotional marketing is called 'brand storytelling' (Quesenberry and Coolsen, 2023).

## Competing in dynamic, global markets

Digital technologies are also enabling organisations to compete in global markets. By utilising data and adapting digital strategies, organisations can target their markets with tailored offerings and communications. Through partnering with others, they are able to reach more markets. At the same time, customers are becoming more aware of, and are seeking, experiences from other countries and cultures. This led to the development of theories of shared values, such as the global consumer culture theory (Arnould and Thompson, 2005, cited in Fill and Turnbull, 2019, p. 34). The theory of GCCT is that the globalisation of markets has led to the emergence of global consumer choice of shared similar beliefs and consumption values – think of global symbols when positioning brands (Kotler and Armstrong, 2020).

## Balancing incremental and radical innovation

As discussed in Chapter 1, the marketing industry requires ever-changing skills. *Prospects* (and now *Jisc*) has been working with the higher education sector for over 40 years, providing a market-led service to offer employment and career guidance to graduates. *Prospects* (2023) advised that *marketing* is a 'a dynamic (one) that's constantly responding to changing consumer habits'. Similarly, the Creative Skillset (2023) has indicated that 'the advertising and marketing industry is one of the most diverse creative industries when it comes to skills, it's difficult to pinpoint the most reliable routes in'.

Although the impact of digital technologies has been influential in opening up marketing opportunities, it can be seen that while they are big issues and change the way things are being done, the importance of the basics of marketing remains. The marketing environment itself, however, is changing rapidly, with technology making new markets easier to reach in a faster time, offering quicker communications with, to, and between different teams and stakeholders, providing masses of information which, if appropriately managed, can offer useful insight. The challenges for marketing educators are to keep up and develop their own practices and pedagogies to match these dynamically changing requirements of the marketing profession.

## THE IMPORTANCE OF INTEGRATED MARKETING COMMUNICATIONS

It is critical, however, that for a marketing process to be successful, every part of the system is communicated clearly to all involved and, in turn, the message of the product or service is ethically presented. As the place of marketing in an organisation has developed, the need for clear communications between the different teams in marketing has increased in importance (Percy, 2023). The requirement for clarity and cohesion has therefore led to the development of marketing communications which has become a specialised part of marketing. This is called integrated marketing communications (IMC). The IMC includes information and promotion, process and imagery, integration, relationships, and experience. Advertising on its own tends towards a 'push' strategy, whereby products are promoted to sell to the customer, while a 'pull'/'profile' strategy is a communication and tactical element of the promotional mix to draw customers (Kotler and Armstrong, 2020; Percy, 2023).

## INSIGHTS FROM AUTHORS' RESEARCH

Previously, in Chapter 1, we provided some of our findings from our research. We'd now like to introduce you to this study and share more about what practitioners think are the key trends in the marketing industry. Dr Dixon-Todd (2019) provides a summary of her research.

## SUMMARY OF THE RESEARCH

Ten participant practitioners were interviewed face-to-face: seven females and three males. All ten were based in the UK. Four were based in the Southeast of England, and seven in the North East of England. They all worked in a marketing communication–related role: three represented relevant professional bodies; six worked in marketing communications roles, including PR-focused, advertising-focused, and marketing-focused; and two specialised in recruiting marketing communications professionals. The participants held various roles, as follows:

Owner, public relations company
Owner, communications recruitment agency
Sales and marketing recruitment consultant
Owner, media and marketing company
Owner, marketing consultancy
CEO, marketing consultancy, and chair of a professional body
Associate director, professional body
Head of external affairs, professional body
Marketing and communications manager
Director of communications and digital

When these individuals were asked about trends, the complexity of the changes was acknowledged, as stated in the following responses.

The CEO of a marketing consultancy and the chair of a professional body identified that things are changing:

> The industry is still attempting to build a new ecosystem, media convergence, fragmentation, and is more complex.

The owner of a communications recruitment agency stated that there are implications for how agencies undertake marketing:

> Some agencies are finding it very difficult to keep up with the changes in the industry as their structures are just not attuned into it. They are structured in a way where working across teams just doesn't work at all. You have a digital team, an engagement team, a financial PR team, a consumer PR team, and a corporate team, and they don't all work together. They may all have a separate profit and loss account, so it's very hard for them to want to work together, because their performance is measured on their profit and loss statements and not on giving their client to another team. So to give away business makes it very difficult.

Another big trend that brings challenges for practitioners is the changing technology and the fast pace of digital transformation. For example, the owner of a marketing consultancy stated:

Technology, adapting to technology. Understanding the benefits but also the harm that can be done. And the belief that technology is 'free' and doesn't need to be managed. Digital – but we're still using the traditional media to signpost the new digital.

The associate director of a professional body agreed and said the challenges are related to 'digital mediums, speed of change, and lack of control in marketing communications'.

The marketing and communications manager also identified these issues and said, 'Fast-paced, more and more on the digital spectrum. It is what it is. Impactful, constantly, constantly evolving, and waiting to see what the next big thing is.'

The owner of a recruitment agency also stressed the move to more content and said, 'More people are doing more content. They might create work in-house, which is media-friendly but content-based.'

These are, indeed, all significant challenges for businesses. There are others brewing that we are yet to really understand, such as the implications of the applied use of artificial intelligence in business. For example, the definition of marketing from the AI system ChatGTP included in Chapter 1 is just the tip of the iceberg. Imagine what else this system could do. Write reports? Strategies? Marketing content? The impact on marketing and marketing education is huge and largely unknown, at present! While the past decade introduced automation and smart machines into manufacturing and production, termed the Industrial Revolution 4.0, IDR4, or just Industry 4.0, the next revolution, Industry 5.0, is already here (Kraagijenbrink, 2023). Many companies are still responding to the impact on business of Industry 4.0 and are not yet able to fully integrate the changes necessitated to now focus on sustainability and corporate responsibility while adapting to the deeper applications of AI across all parts of marketing and business (Hunt, 2018). With the focus on machine learning, Internet of Things, and artificial intelligence, marketers must be ready to adapt their way of working, or they will be left behind in the new age of new teamwork between humans and machines (Kraagijenbrink, 2023).

**FIGURE 2.14** Digital marketing image.

## IMPLICATIONS FOR PRACTICE: INFLUENCES AND DISRUPTION IN MARKETING

As marketing has developed, there have been both influences and disruption in how products and processes are sold to the customers/consumers. In terms of companies promoting their products internationally, there are other influences to consider. As noted earlier in PESTEL, for organisations working in an international and global market, there are many considerations to take into account, such as the language differences, symbols and religion, values, beliefs, standardisation, or adaption. Even if a campaign is in one country, given the global nature or media, communications can be viewed across many different countries. How products/brands are received varies between cultures and ethnic identities. So the artwork/pictures on a poster within a campaign must be respectful to all different belief systems, especially for any online promotions (Kotler and Armstrong, 2020).

Although many organisations research the context and country well, even small errors can be costly and, worse, offensive (Kotler and Armstrong, 2020). While many global brands have been successful and produced strong campaigns, such as Proctor & Gamble (P&G), Heineken, and Unilever, many more have failed, such as Canadian company Food Basics, which had the good intention of promoting a product to celebrate Baisakhi but presented the food inappropriately for Sikhs (Fill and Turnbull, 2019, p. 33). This is where standardisation, while cost-effective, may not always meet local tastes or cultures, whereas adapting does. Adaptation, therefore, takes into account different cultural environments of each market but is exceedingly a complex strategic choice. Some organisations adopt a strategy of 'glocalisation'; this means that the organisation develops a global platform centrally but allows local markets to adapt or localise the communications/product to fit (Percy, 2023).

Internationalisation and globalisation of business mean all companies must endeavour to be responsible for the impact of their business on the world around them. As noted earlier in the external environment, the place of corporate social responsibility has therefore grown in importance, and this, too, means marketing strategies must be sustainable and respond to the goals noted in the United Nations (2023) pledge, which states that:

> The Sustainable Development Goals are a call for action by all countries – poor, rich, and middle-income – to promote prosperity while protecting the planet. They recognize that ending poverty must go hand-in-hand with strategies that build economic growth and address a range of social needs including education, health, social protection, and job opportunities, while tackling climate change and environmental protection. More important than ever, the goals provide a critical framework for COVID-19 recovery.

The implications around ensuring sustainable marketing strategies are further discussed in subsequent chapters. In terms of responding to the current trends in marketing as discussed previously, Dr Andrew Kristoffer Dean said that:

> At present, there is an overt drive to embed AI into marketing, but this is just the beginning. When marketers better embrace the fact that we are embodied beings, the next revolution will be pharmacological, neuroscientific, and genetic.

Benjamin Spence is researching marketing practice and said that:

> From a research perspective, several brands appear to be engaging with cause-related marketing and externally promoting their corporate social responsibility initiatives. This, as many brands have found, is not as simple as creating a rainbow-adapted logo for Pride Month or a one-off charitable donation to tick a box. Entering the realm of promoting your brand as inclusive or one which is mindful of the environment, for example, invites scrutiny from consumers on the brand's internal and external operations, mission statements, partner organisations, and historical activity. This can lead to the brand not only being labelled as 'rainbow washing', 'sports washing', and 'green washing', for example, by the demographic in which they are trying to reach but also risk being labelled as 'woke washing' from their core demographic.

## TASKS

### Task 2.1

Imagine you are working as a marketing manager in your selected industry. Identify the key threats and opportunities.

### Task 2.2

Research what is meant by Industry 5.0, and consider how this might impact those working in marketing.

## SUMMARY OF CHAPTER 2

In this chapter, the changing nature of marketing and how it has adapted to the challenges of the internal and external environment was discussed. The importance of the management of a company designing business and marketing strategies that are operationally feasible in both macroenvironmental and microenvironmental terms was then further examined. In order to continue to grow their business, marketing management must secure and respond to accurate data that will show the demographic, economic, and natural environment. The role of a PESTLE analysis to achieve this aim was also presented.

## REFERENCES

Advertising Standards Agency. (2023) Available from: Home – ASA | CAP.
American Marketing Association. (2023a) *Content Marketing*. Available from: American Marketing Association | AMA.

American Marketing Association. (2023b) *7 Big Problems in the Marketing Industry* | American Marketing Association – DC (amadc.org).

Boyd, E.H. (2023) *State of the Environment: Health, People, and the Environment.* Environment Agency. Available from: State of the environment: Health, people and the environment – GOV.UK (www.gov.uk).

Chartered Institute of Marketing (CIM). (2023) Available from: www.cim.co.uk/.

Cole, G.A. and Kelly, P. (2015) *Management. Theory and Practice.* 8th Edition. Hampshire: Cengage Learning.

Creative Skillset. (2023) Available from: https://rts.org.uk/tags/creative-skillset.

Fill, C. and Turnbull, S. (2019) *Marketing Communications.* Harlow: Pearson.

Gov.UK. (2023) *The UK's Trade Agreements.* Available from: The UK's trade agreements – GOV.UK (www.gov.uk).

Hague, P.N., Harrison, M., Cupman, J. and Truman, O. (2016) *Market Research in Practice: An Introduction to Gaining Greater Market Insight.* London: Kogan Page.

Hunt, S.D. (2018) Advancing marketing strategy in the marketing discipline and beyond: From promise, to neglect, to prominence, to fragment (to promise?). *Journal of Marketing Management,* 34(1–2), 16–51. https://doi.org/10.1080/0267257X.2017.1326973.

Kraagijenbrink, J. (2022) *What Is Industry 5 and How Will It Radically Change Your Business Strategy?* Available from: What Is Industry 5.0 And How It Will Radically Change Your Business Strategy? (forbes.com) (Accessed 1 May 2023).

Orazi, D.C., Spry, A., Theilacker, M.N. and Vredenburg, J. (2017) A multi-stakeholder IMC framework for networked brand identity. *European Journal of Marketing,* 51(3), 551–571. https://doi.org/10.1108/EJM-08-2015-0612.

Prospects. (2023) Available from: Who we are | Prospects.ac.uk.

Smart Insights. (2023) *RACE Digital Planning Framework.* Available from: RACE Planning Framework | Smart Insights.

Trading Economics. (2023) Available from: https://tradingeconomics.com/united-kingdom/inflation-cpi.

United Nations. (2023) *Sustainable Development Goals.* Available from: www.un.org/sustainabledevelopment/sdg-media-compact-about/.

Whittington, R., Regner, P., Angwin, D., Johnson, G. and Scholes, K. (2020) *Exploring Strategy. Text and Cases.* Harlow: Pearson Education.

## RECOMMENDED FURTHER READING

Kotler, P.T. and Armstrong, G. (2020) *Principles of Marketing.* 18th Edition. Harlow: Pearson.
*Authors' comment: Kotler and Armstrong have updated their accessible classic work*
Percy, L. (2023) *Strategic Integrated Marketing Communications.* Abingdon: Routledge.
*Authors' comment: Percy provides a clear insight into the critical role of IMC in current marketing practice.*
Quesenberry, K.A. and Coolsen, M.K. (2023) *Brand Storytelling. IMC for a Digital Landscape.* London: Rowman and Littlefield.

## CHAPTER 3

# Introducing management
*Theory to practice*

## SYNOPSIS AND LEARNING OUTCOMES

At the end of this chapter, successful students will be able to do the following:

1. Demonstrate an appreciation of theories of leadership and management to enable the application of the principles of management within a given context.

2. Apply appropriate project management and marketing tools to the procurement of a warehouse and a vegetarian shop and café and the launch of the opening of the respective new venue.

## INTRODUCTION

In this chapter, we will review some leading management and leadership theorists whose work has influenced the management of marketing and business to the present day. While you may have studied management theorists in detail in attaining a previous qualification, the purpose of this chapter is to highlight some key aspects of management theory that may act as a reminder and be helpful to you in deciding how best to develop your skills for your marketing career.

We have divided the chapter into three sections. The first section starts with an outline of the purpose of management and presents some insights into key theorists who have influenced methods of management across a variety of sectors. We then explore some aspects of leadership that are critical to leading and managing roles in a marketing context. Remember, every business must be led, managed, and marketed! In Section 2, we provide an overview of basic project management and how it can be applied to a planned marketing activity that follows in Section 3, which also provides a chapter summary.

DOI: 10.4324/9781003365136-3

## SECTION 1

### What is *management*?

*Management* can be described as the organisation and coordination of activities that can be involved in any aspect of life, from business to healthcare to charities or government. The management process is described by Witzel (2022, p. 1) as 'the coordination and direction of activities of oneself and others towards some particular end'. The management process may sound simple, but it is an exceedingly complex process that has been studied for many years. Early studies on improving processes started in engineering in the early twentieth century with research called 'scientific management', such as Frederick Taylor's seminal work *The Principles of Scientific Management* (1947). He was the first to really study the nature of work (Drucker, 1974). Frederick Winslow Taylor was an American Quaker engineer who invented scientific management, which was the foundation of later work in time and motion studies. He began work as a labourer in the steel industry, progressing to chief engineer, whereby he started breaking down tasks into small sections, utilising a stopwatch to see how long things took and whether or not, with various adjustments, tasks could be done more

**FIGURE 3.15** Management meeting.

efficiently. His study 'scientific management' was the forerunner to time and motion studies developed by Frank and Lillian Gilbreth (1917). In the early 1900s, Henry Ford also applied standardised processes to the assembly line at the Ford Motor plant (Jenson, 1989). This has become known as 'Fordism' as a management style, a term used by several management theorists. While effective results were demonstrated, the impact was not so good on people, as the tasks were repetitive, with a lack of human interaction. Max Weber further examined machine-like authority in bureaucratic administration systems and stressed the importance of control and authority through rules, regulations, and procedures (1930).

Over the years of management research, the scientific models of management were replaced by human relations models, as management researchers presented evidence to show that the human aspect was critically important, whereby the values of commitment, participation, and openness started to appear. Mayo (1949) is recognised as the forerunner in developing human relations theory and applying it to industry. Elton W. Mayo was an Australian-born medical student who specialised in mental and moral philosophy, with a particular interest in industrial sociology, firstly teaching in the United Kingdom, then moving to the United States to work at Harvard University. His renowned research is known as the Hawthorne studies, named after his research into Western Electric's Hawthorne Works in Chicago. Mayo led a team of scientists from Harvard University to instigate changes to working conditions, involving employees in the process; he was then able to demonstrate that appreciating employees' emotions, showing respect, and creating working peer groups at work would lead to better working relationships and productivity. Mary Parker Follett (1868–1933) was one of the early management theorists to recognise the importance of ethical, humanistic management, and also, Chester I. Barnard (1886–1961) equally recognised the importance of the informal aspects of an organisation, such as cliques and friendship and interest groups (Follett and Barnard, cited in Daft and Bensen, 2015, p. 44). The body of knowledge on applied management theories has grown therefore exponentially over the past hundred years (see *inter alia*: Handy, 1976; Schein, 1985).

The human relationship model of management, recognising the social influences and importance for employees, has therefore expanded since Mayo's (1949) studies from the idea that employees are motivated not just by money but by a range of factors, such as a sense of belonging and commitment to the success of the organisation. Mayo (1949) was not against authority and control but argued for more flexibility in management. Flexible and open systems of management have developed over the decades that emphasise diversity, innovation, adaptation, growth, and the inclusion of employees in decisions around resource acquisition (Covey, 1989; Byrd and Sparkman, 2022).

The success of any management strategy, of course, depends on the approach taken by the managers. Managers are very different in personality and in management style and take various approaches in deciding how to conduct their role. Regardless of the style of management they adopt, they have to carry out the role of managers generally, which means they are responsible for the fulfilment of the application of the organisation's strategy, whether it is a business or in a different setting, such as in a hospital or charity. The larger the organisation, of course, the more sections/departments there will be that will require a manager. The manager will have responsibility for each aspect of the strategy, from the ethical working of the company to the knowledge of the organisation, to the capital and finances and the employees. Charles Handy's early studies of management, published in

*Understanding Organisations* (1976), *The Future of Work* (1984, 1986), and *The Making of Managers* (1988), have been widely influential in business because he took into account the requirement of managers to respond to rapid change on a daily basis. Handy (1990) was able to develop his views on how best to manage change, and he further examines it in his later work, *The Age of Unreason*, whereby he was able to predict the dynamic influences of digital technologies.

How a manager may conduct their daily business has therefore been the research topic of many business experts. For example, Henry Mintzberg (1973) and Warren Bennis (1989) were two of the early researchers to analyse the complexity and diversity of the manager's role (Witzel, 2022, page 4). To conduct his research, Mintzberg (1973) spent time in different-sized organisations, observing how managers spent their time, and noted that successful managers could cope well with ambiguity. Warren Bennis (1989) was an American industrial psychologist and adviser to four presidents and famously said, 'Managers do things right. Leaders do the right thing' (quoted in Covey, 1989, p. 101). The research studies at this time sought to clarify and analyse the nature of the manager's role, and a number of practical lists of activities were identified.

One of the early management theorists to stress the importance of marketing in business management was German-born Theodore Levitt. While he was working at Harvard Business School, his research findings, the *Marketing Myopia*, published in 1960, argued that every industry must grow and its primary aim should be to satisfy customers rather than to simply be a goods production organisation. Levitt recognised the critical role marketing plays in managing organisations, and the importance of effective marketing has grown ever since the 1980s (Levitt, 1983).

Another important pathfinder is Henry Fayol, who was a French mining engineer and is acknowledged as being one of the first to ask the question, 'What is management?' Fayol's (1949) research findings showed the links between organisational strategy, management, and leadership development. The empirical findings by Fayol have laid the foundation for a deeper understanding of the importance of authentic management and leadership. Peter Drucker, born in Vienna (1946), is also recognised as a leading lifelong contributor to management theories, whereby throughout his work, Drucker (1974) states the importance of objective-setting to ensure the effectiveness of managers. Both Peter Drucker (1974) and Henri Fayol (1984) identified five broad criteria of management tasks that are as important today as in earlier times. They can be broadly summarised as follows:

1. Planning strategies and objectives
2. Creating systems and organising
3. Communicating and motivating employees
4. Coordinating activities
5. Measuring effectiveness against costs

Each aspect of the manager's role has been extensively studied, and a vast body of knowledge has been accumulated, so we highlight in what follows some of the key aspects of the theories related to the importance of the key management tasks as noted by Fayol (1984) and Drucker (1974).

## Planning strategies and objectives

Many businesses have a mission statement; think, for example, of the different slogans you have perhaps seen in marketing campaigns. Designing planning strategies and objectives will start with the company's goals. The goals relate to how the mission is to be accomplished, and then the strategic objectives are designed and planned. Any strategy involves options and restraints of ethics, time, and costs. Simply, when designing a strategy, 'there are usually three basic options, – do this, do something else, or do nothing – and usually there are many more than that' (Witzel, 2022, p. 13).

The study of the complexity of business strategy has origins in the military sciences, with early fifth/sixth-century writings such as Sun Tzu's *The Art of War* influencing the military and later being reproduced to apply to strategic business tactics (Gagliardi and Tzu, 2014). Also, for example, the early writings in the sixteenth century of the political writer Nicolo Machiavelli formed the foundation of some ideas of how the basic aspects of strategic planning proposed by Machiavelli could be applied to business (Witzel, 2022).

One of the major contributors to analyse the complexity of forming and undertaking strategic goals was the Canadian academic Henry Mintzberg (1993). He realised how time, the environment, and the impact of competing variables meant managers were always having to settle between less-than-perfect strategic choices. This aspect of uncertainty led to Igor Ansoff (1965) developing a model of what he termed 'environmental turbulence'. Ansoff (1965) created a three-dimensional scale to ascertain the level of turbulence, which were instability, discontinuity, and unpredictability. This, or a similar model, can help managers decide the impact of potential risks of a particular strategic implementation and, of course, how to best structure a business or a marketing plan.

One of the best-known sets of generic strategies, still employed today, are those developed by Michael Porter (1980). Professor Porter believed that all businesses have just four basic options to adopt – cost leadership, differentiation, cost focus, and focused differentiation – and basically have to decide whether to sell to a mass or a small market and then plan the appropriate steps in the strategy. In marketing terms, Porter himself became his own 'brand' after his first book, *Competitive Strategy* (1980), sold so many copies it became acknowledged at that time as the definitive work on corporate strategy. When he joined Harvard University, he was an early supporter of placing corporate strategy within a market, stating that a company's competitive advantage must be analysed by taking into consideration five factors:

1. Existing rivalry between firms
2. The threat of new entrants to a market
3. The threat of substitute products and services
4. The bargaining power of suppliers
5. The bargaining power of buyers

Porter (1980) identified a further five generic descriptions of industries – fragmented, emerging, mature, declining, and global – noting that within these generic aspects were two kinds of competitive advantage: low cost and differentiation. From this foundational study of companies, Porter (1990) then went on to design Porter's diamond theory of national advantage of four points basically: factor conditions; demand conditions; firm strategy, structure, and rivalry; and related and supporting industries.

Porter (1990) showed how competitive a company could be if they analysed their 'value chain', which is how effective all its activities are. If the value chain was working well, their strategic planning would support their competitive advantage.

As argued by Chris Argyris (1985), however, many strategies fail, especially if they are causing considerable change, because employees have not been kept fully informed. Argyris (1985) terms this 'defensive routines'. So a large part of a manager's role is to ensure any strategy is carefully communicated to employees.

## Creating systems and organising

Different structures of organisations have led to quite diverse theories of how they function. Some theorists suggest organisations are like machines, but as noted by Burrell and Morgan (1979) and Mintzberg (1993), while structures may be similar, no two organisations are the same, and in terms of management of an organisation, this is frequently not machine-like and may be quite imperfect. Alfred D. Chandler, an economic historian, was the Straus professor at Harvard University, and his most influential analysis was on the relationship between strategy and structure in organisations (Chandler, 1962). He studied the implications of positive and defensive strategies in large organisations, showing how entrepreneurial strategies around new markets were positive and led to success, whereas defensive strategies had negative results when a company tried to protect its role in the market. His work highlighted the importance of coordinated strategies in response to outside pressures.

Of course, there are many different types of companies, and they all require structured systems and organisation, and the way in which they operate fascinated two influential writers: Tom Peters and Peter Waterman, who were employed by the management firm McKinsey when they published their book *In Search of Excellence* in 1982, which proved very popular and became a bestseller. In the book, they reported how 43 excellent companies had performed against the famous McKinsey 'Seven-S' formula they had developed: structure, strategy, systems, style of management, skills (corporate strengths), staff, and shared values. They used their research to analyse an organisation's success against these seven metrics. When, five years after the book was first published, many of the 'excellent' companies had actually failed, Peters and Waterman argued that only by exploring how to continually improve and meet the demands of unplanned change could organisations survive. They further argued in their follow-up book, *Thriving on Chaos* (1988), that to stay viable in a fast-changing world, it would be necessary to restructure to a horizontal, rather than a hierarchical, management structure. Peters and Waterman also emphasised the importance of corporate culture and values and the strategic management of change, which remains central to the success of companies today. At the same time, as *In Search of Excellence* was popular in management literature, Kenichi Ohmae, the head of Mckinsey's Tokyo office, brought Japanese management style to Western cultures in his influential books *The Mind of the Strategist* (1982) and *Triad Power* (1985). Ohmae's strategy was to ask 'why' repeatedly throughout strategic preparations. He drew on successful Japanese companies, such as Toyota and Honda, to share his views of successful organisations and argued that business strategy is based on the 'art of strategic thinking' and building successful strategies within the reality of the environment (1982). In terms of marketing, Ohmae recognised a competitive advantage exists when the full expectations of the customer are acknowledged and supported the 'just-in-time' ordering of components for the production line utilised by Taiichi Ohno at Toyota (Ohmae, 1985).

While other types of organisations may be bureaucratic in style, they still have a place in modern society. For example, a bureaucratic system works well in government, colleges and universities, police, and fire departments. A criticism of bureaucracies, however, is that they may be slow or difficult to change; while Peters and Waterman (1988) argued that bureaucracies are not as effective as they could be, Handy (1990) took the view that too much change is itself problematic.

If you consider the process of government, many different departments are involved in undertaking the various aspects of ensuring a country operates successfully. To do this, there will be organised systems of communications and technology. This is where a bureaucratic structure is most effective, because there is a clear chain of command, and individual roles and responsibilities are clearly defined. Other types of organisational structures favour functional, flat, matrix, or multidivisional structures, and the type of structure varies depending on the nature of the organisation and the internal and external environment. Described as 'open systems', for a company to respond rapidly to changes, it must be flexible and responsive, defined as 'organic' by Burns and Stalker (1961).

However, businesses will have an organisation chart that shows the managers and their teams. In a large company, the organisational chart would have a board of directors at the top, followed by lines of communications and responsibility, depending on the number of networks and departments. In other words, the operation of any business or enterprise would encompass different systems and organisation. For example, a human resource strategy would be applied by specialist human resources management and employees, while a marketing strategy would consider how best to promote goods. You will have seen in previous chapters how important it is to ensure that the various aspects of marketing are inter-linked through effective communications.

Another organisational model important today is that of the family business or the family model of business; of course, these businesses are 'personality driven' for the most part, meaning, that how they operate is heavily dependent on the personality or personalities of the family member(s) running the company or business. Dyer (1986), in his seminal work, identified seven general leadership cultures that are today commonly referred to as the family firm leadership styles: autocratic, expert, laissez-faire, participative, referent, transactional, and transformational. Examining management styles in family-run businesses is beyond the scope of this book, but if you are interested in pursuing this issue further, please see the literature review by Fries et al. (2021).

## Communicating and motivating employees

Good communication is vital for a manager to be able to motivate employees. While the most successful companies site clear and open communication as vital to their success, ensuring smooth communication is not without difficulties. For example, it may be that the desired communication gets mixed up or gets distorted as it passes through a number of different channels in the hierarchy of the organisation.

Communication is often described as vertical, through the layers of the hierarchy, or horizontal, between different departments. Coordination, rather than control, is what managers do to ensure everyone understands their role in the organisation (Witzel, 2022). Successful managers keep the lines of communication open; you will recall from Chapters 1 and 2 how important marketing communications is and how someone encodes the message, but as discussed, someone may misunderstand the message! A key part of a manager's role, therefore, is how they organise communication channels.

Motivating employees is a key aspect of management in order to enable the organisation to achieve its aims and objectives. Different theories of motivation have been developed, such as Maslow's hierarchy of needs theory (1970), McGregor's theory X/theory Y (1960), or Herzberg's, Mausner's, and Snyderman's (1959) hygiene factors and motivators. We explore their influence and impact in more detail in Chapter 8, when we examine the challenges of leading and managing teams.

## Coordinating activities

A key aspect of a manager's role is coordination, which is ensuring each part of the organisation's business works smoothly. The manager will have to ensure the employees work within their remit, and within and across teams and departments. The coordination of activities is usually reflected in the responsibility lines in the organisation charts.

## Measuring effectiveness against costs

The manager must perhaps start with the current performance of the company and ask basic questions related to its purpose. Is it working? What are its strengths and weaknesses (see 'strengths, weaknesses, opportunities, and threats' (SWOT) in the project management section). What is important to prioritise, and why?

For example, 'knowledge' is critical to business, so what aspects of specific information are critical to the business that is being managed? Information the manager must know is conveyed by means of data, while knowledge is relative to the specific business and contingent on that data. Hard data, for example, profit margins, and soft data, for example, assumptions, expectations or speculation, and so on, will result in overall trends that provide general impressions of the business environment. Knowledge management focuses on how to deliberately create and use knowledge more efficiently, for example, the use of information communications technology. A frequent saying used in management is, 'We must look again at the data', but what they really mean is, 'Look again at what information the data is showing'. Tacit and explicit knowledge distinctions were made by Michael Polanyi in the 1950s (Polanyi, [1958] 1974) and developed by knowledge theorists Nonaka Ikujiro and Hirotaka Takeuchi (1995) and Max Boisot (1998). *Explicit knowledge* is knowledge that we can easily formulate or write down and pass onto others in the terminology of knowledge management; *explicit knowledge* is easily codified and often based on provable factual data and on reason. Explicit knowledge can be easily communicated, for example, in how to write a marketing plan, whereas tacit knowledge is very personable and hard to formulate and express. In a good marketing plan, the competent leader may have a clear vision of their strategy and be able to translate it to the manager and the marketing team. A cohesive marketing team may feel they know what they are doing, but this may not make sense to another team. The leadership and marketing team are then basing their plan on soft data and intuition. Explicit knowledge is telling and showing something, but tacit knowledge is how it 'feels' to really practice management. Ensuring that knowledge of data is accurate is critical to financial management.

Financial management is a complex subject and is viewed as an academic subject requiring professional training. Although corporate finance is a highly specialised subject, basically, however, any company must manage its finances. The management accounting function looks at costs and income or revenue. Costs will include everything the business has to spend to operate, from rent for a building to staff and capital costs. Management accounting consists of a key planning process, and budgets are allocated for each aspect and will include some financial accounting. In large companies, management accounting and financial accounting are separate, specialised processes that may be carried out by large departments. These specialist functions include taking care of the accounts inside the company, while financial accounting focuses on the outside and prepares information for the shareholders, debtholders, regulatory bodies, and government tax authorities. Companies are legally required to employ independent auditors to check their accounts for accuracy. The moral and legal requirement to manage money responsibly is part of the role of the management team of the company.

## Summary of management roles and human resources

As noted by Mintzberg (1989), management roles can be broadly divided into three categories: interpersonal, informational, and decisional. Within this context, Mintzberg (1994) also identified three ways that managers can ensure work gets done in their organisation: they could do the work themselves (hands-on) or lead or control others through information (administration). The choice and the way this is undertaken varies very much dependent on the type of organisation and the manager's own managerial style (Brewer, 1991). Different responses to requests within the context of management style also vary. For example, if an employee asks a manager a question, the manager's answer will vary depending on the type of role they usually adopt. For example, as a 'communicator', to a request for information: 'Finance has some data on that. Please check with them.' Alternatively, as a 'doer', they may say, 'Leave it with me'. As a 'controller', they may refuse to answer the question, while as a leader, they may respond by redirecting the question back to the employee: 'What do you feel/think?' The employee may then feel unsatisfied with the response! So communication again could go astray, while staff feelings of uncertainty could lead to resistance. To avoid this happening, it is as important for managers as it is for employees to have clearly defined roles: the 'how' the roles are played is critical to business success. Human resource management (HRM) has a role to help the organisation work effectively, so a function of HRM is to assist managers in designing job descriptions that are appropriate for the requirements of the role. In the past, managers used to have a strong HR function, frequently termed a 'personnel' function, but since the 1950s, the work of human resources has become a much wider, strategy-developing role, a key function of which would be acting within Employment Law (2023) and then identifying, recruiting, and nurturing talented employees so that a competitive advantage can be secured through the implementation of three major organisational strategic tasks, identified by Bartlett and Ghoshal (2002, p. 37) as the following:

Building (HR systems, processes, and culture)
Linking (developing social networks vital to knowledge management)
Bonding (creating a sense of identity and belonging)

The employment relationship with all staff is therefore critical to the success of an organisation, and the way this is achieved in a positive manner is very much the key to a manager being successful in managing the organisation's business strategy.

A marketing manager needs to have strong interpersonal skills and be able to portray a 'figurehead' role in terms of their knowledge of how best to promote and manage a product or service. If they have led the successful development and promotion of a product, a service, or a company, this would help their role as a leader and make liaising and communicating with their employees much more successful. The complexity of the role of management, in any sphere, means that the informational aspects of their role include monitoring, evaluating, and disseminating information. To do this effectively, the manager would need to be able to make decisions on matters that arise from a cross section of the organisation's business activities. The nature of the decisions to be made depend on the type of business, of course, but good decision-making is a learned skill, as becoming a good manager can only be learned through trial and error!

This view was supported by Peter Coleman (2023).

## CASE STUDY 3.1

### *Peter Coleman*

Peter worked in senior management in operations across a number of sectors, including the automobile industry. He also introduced manufacturing operations from greenfield sites while project-managing new technology in the UK from Japan. While Peter was working as a senior manager in operations, his approach to production and operations systems management was influenced by Taylor's scientific management theory (1947) and the strategic methods of production of the Japanese as applied by Ohmae (1985) in Toyota and Honda. However, in terms of applied theorists on managing people, Peter said, in his career, it was very much a case of 'learning on the job', and he learned his own management style from a 'pick and mix' approach, whereby he observed the results and respect gained by some managers and not by others. Peter moved from industry to higher education and is completing his PhD in 2023. His research explores the benefits of improving 'core competencies' in small and medium enterprises (SMEs) whilst allowing for greater exporting of goods. The work is titled *A Case Study of Northeast England's Manufacturing Firms*.

We also note in what follows our own views of the qualities required to succeed in management.

**FIGURE 3.16** Group of three students working together.

### The authors' personal views of what constitutes a 'good manager'

Over the years in our own employment, the authors have worked for a number of different managers, in marketing, other international business environments, and higher education. Here is a summary of our personal views of what knowledge, skills, and qualities are valuable in a good marketing manager. We have summarised the qualities into three levels, with level 3 being the desired level, and levels 2 and 1 being required but not as important as level 3. We start with the ideal manager at level 3:

### *Knowledge, skills, and personality traits*

Level 3: Marketing manager – knowledge, skills, and personality traits

*Knowledge and skills*

A good marketing manager is able to create a relaxing, non-critical environment for his/her team in which they can brainstorm marketing strategies and ideas for new or existing markets and for new or existing products and/or services.

They are adept at conflict resolution, either within his/her team or with other company departments, or with external suppliers, customers, or clients.

They are skilled in:

1. Bargaining and negotiating, for example, in contract negotiations when outsourcing different marketing functions, such as graphic design or product labelling and packaging, or when agreeing to terms of transportation contracts.

2. Identifying new markets for the company's/business's product(s) and/or service(s).

3. Identifying how the company's/business's product(s) and/or service(s) can be enhanced to provide a competitive advantage in its respective market(s).

4. Knowing when to delegate responsibilities and authority to his/her marketing team or groups in order to meet project deadlines. (For example, in large companies with a diverse product line or portfolio of services, a marketing team can comprise several smaller groups.)

5. Recognizing people's different personalities and areas of expertise, knowledge, and experience so he/she can create a well-functioning team or individual groups.

They should be knowledgeable about body language and the non-verbal clues (i.e. body posture, stance, and facial expressions) that people display, which can show their true emotions and feelings and therefore may be in conflict to what they are actually saying. This is a useful skill to have with reference to conflict resolution and to points 1 and 5 earlier.

He/she should also possess the knowledge and skills outlined in level 1: knowledge and business skills and level 2: marketer knowledge and skills, which follow.

### Key personality traits

However, even though a person may possess the relevant knowledge and business skills (level 1) and marketer knowledge and skills (level 2), he/she may still not make a good marketing manager without certain key personality traits.

A good manager should be assertive but not aggressive, and conciliatory but not argumentative.

They should be:

- Able to adapt quickly to changing circumstances and 'can think on his/her feet'.

- A good communicator and be an active listener.

- Able to inspire trust, confidence, and loyalty in those that they manage.

- Willing to accept solutions to problems at all times from those he/she manages if their proposed solution to a problem is better for the company/business than his/hers and be magnanimous in those situations.

- A good coach at times, able to impart their knowledge and expertise to help those they manage in their everyday tasks.

- Blessed with strong powers of persuasion, whether it is in regard to actual marketing strategies or in regard to the team, for example, when persuading their team to work overtime when needed in order to meet project deadlines.

A good manager should be 'proactive', that is, able to foresee potential difficulties or problems ahead of time so steps can be taken to avoid a difficulty or solve a problem promptly, and not be 'reactive', that is, the so-called 'firefighting' style of management, when action is only taken when difficulties/problems manifest themselves.

## Level 2: marketer – knowledge and skills

In the same way as the ideal manager (level 3), the marketer needs to develop a thorough knowledge of marketing strategies and how they can be applied in the marketplace.

They should:

- Strive to keep informed of competitors or potential competitors and the product(s) and/or service(s) they provide in the employer's present/potential market(s.)

And be skilled in:

- Employing basic marketing strategies in order to promote the company's/business's product(s) and/or service(s).

- Identifying the strengths and weaknesses of the company or business (ref. 'SWOT' analysis).

- Recognising the opportunities and threats that confront the company/business in the marketplace (ref. 'SWOT' analysis).

### Key personality traits

The marketer should be able to work well in groups and be familiar with the theory of 'group dynamics', in that sometimes an individual will take the leadership role in a group and at other times he/she will be a worker/follower in a group.

They should be aware of some of the psychological frameworks that are employed in marketing, such as Maslow's hierarchy of needs (1970), which is a psychological marketing tool to help marketers target their products/services to the appropriate needs of buyers.

The marketer should also possess the knowledge and skills outlined in level 1: knowledge and business skills, outlined next.

### Level 1: knowledge and business skills

He/she should:

- Have competent skills in communication (both in the spoken and written word).
- Have effective time management skills so that they can manage their time carrying out their everyday tasks in order to meet team/group or individual project deadlines.
- Possess adequate problem-solving skills, as due to the dynamic nature of the marketing environment, problems can manifest themselves suddenly, and the ability to provide solutions in a timely manner is essential.

### Key personality traits

They will have good 'interpersonal' skills, that is, the skills we use when communicating and dealing with others in the workplace, involving our attitude and behaviour towards co-workers and managers.

### Exploring your own knowledge, skills, and personality traits

After considering the development of management practice as noted earlier, how would you answer the following questions?

1. Are you a good listener?
2. As a manager, do you avoid interrupting others, especially those junior to you?
3. Are you good at sensing how the other person feels today, by picking up on non-verbal clues (such as body language)?

Perhaps make some notes in response to the preceding questions; you will be able to refer back to them in later chapters when you are invited to review your own knowledge and skills for a marketing career.

At level 1, a manager will be proficient in numeracy and computer literacy; for example, he/she/they can use word processors, spreadsheets, and graphic design software and will be competent using search engines and AI applications, such as ChatGPT, for marketing research purposes.

The manager will have general knowledge of finance and be familiar with terms such as *fixed* and *variable costs, break-even point, gross profit*, and *net profit*.

Can you think about where you may need to expand your own knowledge and skills? We will explore how to do this in more detail in Chapter 7. A good manager, of course, will have leadership skills, as an effective leader will also be an influential manager. The next section discusses some aspects of effective leadership.

**FIGURE 3.17** Two students walking and chatting.

## Leadership in management

We explore theories of leadership and how you can apply leadership skills in more detail in terms of personal reflection in Chapter 9, so in this section of the chapter, we highlight some aspects of leadership that are part of a manager's role.

The manager's role does include leadership, particularly in terms of setting a clear direction for the company and ensuring employees share in the company's vision. A key leading function for a manager in any company is to lead employees in terms of motivation and commitment, to ensure the organisation's stated aims and objectives are achieved (Combe, 2014).

Leadership and management knowledge and skills coalesce in project management, so the next section of the chapter outlines some key aspects of successfully managing projects.

## SECTION 2

### Project management

A project is not easily defined simply because they are so diverse in nature. This is because, for example, if you consider what is required within the context of different projects, the requirements for planning an event will be markedly different to those necessary for building an extension to an existing building. In simple terms, a project can be described as a structured undertaking that requires resources and planning, and it has a beginning and an end. In the same way as management and leadership have witnessed the development of a range of theories about what criteria are important, the diversity of project management has also accumulated a similar vast body of knowledge. In this section of the chapter, we will look at some of the major aspects of project management so that you can choose how to plan different marketing projects.

## What is a *project*?

Managing a project is different from managing people, so we start this introduction by exploring a basic project. To start with, how could you view the project? What is different about the project from normal, day-to-day working? A *project* is usually defined as something that has a start and an end. A basic project starts with a definition; it's then planned and organised, undertaken, and finished. Prior to starting on the project itself, you would complete a feasibility study/report, which, depending on the size of the project, can be a complex undertaking. The aim of the feasibility study is simply to decide if the project is viable or not.

## The feasibility study/report

The viability of the project is explored during the feasibility study. You would define exactly what the project is and if there is a need for it, then you would check to make sure you had the capital, resources, material, and people to undertake it. As you can imagine, the bigger the project, the more detailed the feasibility study needs to be. The subsequent report would demonstrate an understanding of the social, technological, ecological, economic, and political (STEEP) factors involved in the proposed project.

The next stage of planning the project is frequently termed a 'project scope'. If you are tasked with this, you would be exploring in detail the full STEEP criteria as noted earlier. To illustrate the requirements of a basic project, we are going to discuss the project management of finding or building a vegetable warehouse for a business-to-business market (B2B).

Ensuring projects run well is not without complexity and challenges. Dr Ryan Williams (2023) works as a project manager and also teaches in universities. Here is what he has to say:.

## CASE STUDY 3.2

### Dr Ryan Williams

When I worked as head of projects, I believed that defining project goals and expectations in cross-departmental projects is an important aspect of project success. Because most organisations are set up to provide business as usual rather than to ensure the success of specific initiatives, the standard methods of identifying project expectations and goals might be ineffective. Even if each division operates according to its own standard operating procedure, cross-departmental cooperation is often necessary for the successful completion of projects.

It's very common for project managers to just bite the bullet and admit that there are too many interdependencies between the teams when working on a shorter project. However, this typically becomes an issue for software projects that are both larger and more sophisticated. In order to guarantee the timely and accurate identification and execution of projects, many businesses employ the use of executive project teams to step in and manage the project's activities as they unfold. Nonetheless, not all businesses can afford to invest in such resources, as they may become expensive and may not necessarily give much value beyond the initial stage of coordinated effort.

Aligning with the corporate goals is a good way to determine which initiatives need to be undertaken. This is different from using a departmental strategy, which has its own goals in mind. When initiatives are identified based on their contributions to corporate goals, rather than through the eyes of individual department heads, execution is streamlined.

The crux of this method is delving into a company strategy to determine what has to be done in the future. After that, initiatives are categorised based on how well they contribute to the company's goals. This streamlines the transition between project and business-as-usual processes.

When reading the following example, as Dr Williams suggests, try to think of how you would categorise the potential project management issues, taking into consideration the vegetable wholesaler's business strategy.

## SECTION 3

### Scoping the project/planning the project

### *Illustration: fictitious case study – an existing fruit and vegetable warehouse wishing to extend*

A wholesale company has a number of fruit and vegetable warehouses and sells its produce directly to trade organisations. It has healthy profit margins and has decided to expand its business into one other region. The feasibility study has been undertaken, and the executive management of the company wants you as project manager to detail (scope) the project in full.

Here is an example of how you would do this.

You would start by breaking down and defining everything that is required. Here are the basic stages and the questions you need to ask:

1.  Is there a business-to-business marketing need for a fruit and vegetable warehouse?
2.  How much is in the budget? You will need to decide on what the budget is and how it will be broken down.

3. What is the time frame?
4. What materials/resources are required, and when are they required?
5. How many people will be involved?
6. Where will you locate the new warehouse?
7. Will you build a new facility or lease/develop an existing warehouse?

## Taking action

To answer the preceding seven basic questions, you will need to collect information to make decisions. You would perhaps review existing buildings that may be suitable for a fruit and vegetable warehouse or build new premises.

## Reviewing existing buildings

To consider the possibility of utilising existing buildings, you would contact commercial estate agents to see what existing premises are for sale. They may also have industrial land for sale or direct you to any of their specialist land agents.

Once you have the brochures with the property particulars, you would conduct a strengths, weaknesses, opportunities, and threats (SWOT) exercise on each of the proposed premises. The use of a simple table or Excel spreadsheet could help here, or using more advanced applications like Microsoft Project or ClickUp, if you feel it is a more complex project.

To perform the SWOT analysis on the properties, you would be looking at the strength of each of the following:

*Geographic location of the warehouse.* Does it have good rail and road access? Close to a city or town where there is a hospitality trade? Where is the warehouse in relation to any competitors?

*Access to the facility.* Is there a parking area suitable for large commercial lorries to manoeuvre? Is there room to create an incoming/outgoing vehicle lane(s)? Simply put, the fact that a lorry driver can turn around a long vehicle easily is a big plus for many customers! Is there access to loading bays? Is the warehouse securely fenced?

*Height and width of the warehouse.* Just as vehicles would require space to move outside, so too is it important for forklift trucks to be able to move safely inside the building.

As well as performing a detailed SWOT on the preceding, other criteria to consider are:

*Stock rotation.* What practical methods of maintaining the fruit and vegetables stock are possible?

*Shelving.* Is there existing shelving suitable for large quantities of boxes of fruit and vegetables?

*Refrigeration.* Is there room for very large commercial refrigeration facilities?

You will also need to consider the location in the warehouse of staff welfare facilities – an office, refreshment, and rest areas.

Once the SWOT is completed on each of the possible buildings, you may identify a suitable building, for example, a warehouse, in the right location for the hospitality trade. It may be that the warehouse was previously used to store/sell crockery and tableware to the same market, so it would not require extensive cleaning to ensure it is safe for produce. In the UK, it would then be necessary to contact the local government in order to complete a registration process for a 'change of use' of the building. However, it may be that there are significant weaknesses in all the available commercial properties, and so you may decide to consider a new build.

## A new building

The specialised estate, or estate and land, agents will have details of land available for sale. In terms of suitability, the same basic principles as noted earlier apply, but in the case of a new build, you may decide to appoint a project manager (PM) to oversee the build and make sure everything is completed within budget and on time. The project manager would make good use of technical tools to monitor and record the development of the building, such as Microsoft Project (Microsoft.com, 2023) or ClickUp (2023). The PM would ensure a full scope of the project, whereby there is a work breakdown structure, statement of work, responsibilities, and full organisational breakdown; furthermore, they would see that a full technical specification is provided, oversee the contract(s) with builders, and facilitate any sub-contracting in order to finish the building. Of course, each aspect would be costed against the finance available for the building of the warehouse. The PM would also need to make a note of any lead time: for example, if goods ordered take six months to arrive, what is it that must take place first, such as a new build? Plus, confirm that other essential steps have been taken, such as ensuring that all the necessary infrastructure has been put in place; otherwise, the project could not take off the ground.

## Launching the new shop and café

From a marketing perspective, we invite you to design the marketing campaign outlined in Chapter 8; however, the purpose of this initial task is for you to consider the management planning aspect of the initial opening of the shop, and the launch of the new business.

You may choose to refer back to Chapters 1 and 2 to decide how to market the launch of the new shop. Here is a reminder of the aspects you may want to consider:

*From the (imaginary) marketing plan of the head office of the vegetarian shop and café (VSC).* Do you need to check any timings/stages of the launch again, and of course, do you need to revise the sum you allocated from your budget?

*Considering the timing of the event.* Has all the marketing mix been finalised (e.g. advertising, prices, and promotion)? Have you prepared the new staff? Is any further training required? Once you have made notes on these points and reviewed the earlier chapters on specialist aspects of marketing, test your knowledge by working through the following task.

## Task 3.1: Launching the new shop and café

Using the vegetarian warehouse project management case study earlier as an example, think about what needs to be done for the launch. How are you going to project-manage the launch of the opening of the new shop and café?

**FIGURE 3.18** Marketing students. Co-workers standing on a stairway.

Why not try to work through this little mnemonic using the word 'marketing' to help you get started?

*M: Message.* For example, methods of advertising product, service, product/service description, sales slogan.
*A: Audience.* For example, identifying target audience/survey content and execution/feedback from surveys affecting product/service development.
*R: Response.* For example, capturing response of customers regarding product/service satisfaction/dissatisfaction.
*K: Competition (OK, not a C but K, but will help you remember! ☺).* For example, other companies providing a similar product/service.
*E: Environment.* For example, barriers to market entry/ethnic, socio-economic, and cultural factors to consider before product/service launch.

*T: Transportation.* For example, sales distribution channels/moving product or delivering service to clients/customers/physical transportation networks and/or cyber networks.

*I: Implementation.* For example, human resources required/target dates for all stages, from research and development through to sales and after-sales service.

*N: Numbers.* For example, raw material and manufacturing costs, administrative costs, cost of product/service trial launch, potential profit margin after identifying fixed and variable costs.

*G: Generation.* For example, generating repeat product sales, generating repeat clients/customers, generating product/service enhancements.

Working through the letters can help you decide how to plan the launch of the shop. Here are some suggestions of what to include in the marketing plan:

How much is in the budget to spend?

How many people in the team are available to work on the launch?

Will you elect a team leader/project manager to coordinate the activities undertaken by each member of the team?

Working backwards from the proposed launch date, what needs to be considered first, and what must be included? Using a simple Excel spreadsheet or applications such as MS Project or ClickUp may help you here.

To ensure you do not miss anything, what about working through the MARKETING mnemonic?

Starting with the letter *M* from 'marketing', what needs to be included in the 'message' about the launch of the new vegetarian shop and café? Remember, you will need to ensure the company's logo is clearly displayed.

## *M: Message*

There so many different ways that companies and businesses advertise their products and/or services nowadays; clearly, their medium of advertising will depend upon whether the advertiser in question is a family-run or small business, a medium-sized company, or a large corporation; business type will therefore dictate the size of their advertising budget and who and where their target audience is. As a reminder as to what has been covered in the previous chapters, these mediums of advertising can probably be divided into five main categories:

*Broadcast advertising.* Such as commercials on radio and television and product placement in movies and TV programs.

*Print advertising.* With advertisements appearing in newspapers or magazines or profession journals and through direct mailing or company/business flyers, which are usually hand-delivered in the case of family-run and small businesses.

*Outdoor advertising.* Where companies and businesses use advertising mediums such as billboards on streets and highways, etc., or advertising on video screens on public transportation.

*Digital advertising.* This covers advertising on websites, via search engines (such as Google and Bing) and through social media advertising (e.g. through platforms such as Facebook and Instagram) and pay-per-click advertising (i.e. this is online advertising, where the advertiser pays a fee every time a user clicks on one of the advertiser's ads).

*Partner company/business referrals.* This is where a pair of companies or businesses enters into a partner agreement where they refer their customers or clients to their partner's company or business. For example, a car rental company refers its customers to a hotel with which it has partnered by giving its customers discount coupons that they can use when they stay at that particular hotel, and vice versa, that is, the hotel gives its customers discount coupons for use with its partner car rental company.

Now move on to the following.

## A: Audience

For example, identifying target audience/survey content and execution/feedback from surveys affecting product/service development.

As noted in previous chapters, *audience* could include the identifying and reaching of target groups, taking into account demographics and social and economic factors, such as household income levels.

## R: Response

For example, capturing the response of customers regarding product/service satisfaction/dissatisfaction.

While you will not be looking at the response to the launch yet, you will need to know the responses of existing or potential customers in order to know what products and food to buy for the new shop. There will be data available from the head office of the vegetarian shop and café. Are you considering any different products for your chosen location?

## K: Competition (OK not a C but K, but will help you remember!)

For example, other companies providing a similar product/service.

You will have checked out the data on your competition from the existing data held by the company, but what are your competitive shops/cafés offering that may impact your shop? You can analyse how the creation of an entirely new market can sometimes change the world of work and leisure. For example, when the personal computer encompassing word processing entered the market, it displaced the typewriter at home and at work and resulted in the end of typing pools in companies!

## E: Environment

For example, barriers to market entry/ethnic, socio-economic, and cultural factors to consider before product/service launch.

This is a vast area. You will need to look at the monopolistic, duopolistic, or oligopolistic power of potential competitor(s)/high capital costs/customer loyalty to existing market participants/regulatory barriers, and so on, utilising the strengths, weaknesses, opportunities, and threats (SWOT) analysis.

### T: Transportation

For example, sales distribution channels/moving product or delivering service to clients/customers via physical transportation networks and/or cyber networks.

For the project management of where to locate the new shop/café, you should have reviewed the availability and transportation and delivery of goods; however, once the shop/café is open, what else could be needed there?

### I: Implementation

For example, human resources required/target dates for all stages, from research and development through to sales and after-sales service.

For implementation, you will need to decide on the staffing levels required for the shop and the café. (We look at this in more detail in Chapter 8.)

### N: Numbers

For example, raw material and manufacturing costs, administrative costs, cost of product/service trial launch, potential profit margin after identifying fixed and variable costs.

In a real situation, you would, of course, look to data held by the head office on the other shops/cafés owned by the shop/café chain to decide what to stock in the short term. With fresh produce, there is of course a limited shelf life, and having vegetable warehouses close by makes it easier to buy more if needed, rather than stock too much that could be wasted.

### G: Generation

For example, generating repeat product sales, generating repeat clients/customers, generating product/service enhancements.

For the new shop/café, your marketing of the launch will generate interest in the new facility. It is then up to the new shop staff to ensure repeat custom!

What else can you add to our earlier example? Keep working through the mnemonic MARKETING until you are sure you have every aspect of the launch of the new shop covered!

## SUMMARY OF CHAPTER 3

In this chapter, we have explored the impact of some key theories of management and leadership on marketing. Of course, there are many more important management theorists whose work has contributed to how successful businesses are today, so you may decide other writers' work is also important to you. Our aim was to highlight some of the leading theorists whose studies have influenced marketing and impacted across a range of sectors. We then explored how organisations are managed and examined some of the issues involved in the role of management.

In the next section of this chapter, we then worked through an illustration of how management and leadership can be exercised in setting up a fictitious new vegetarian shop and café (VSC). In the next part of the book, that is, Book Section 2, we discuss how to develop a career in marketing.

# REFERENCES

Ansoff, H.I. (1965) *Corporate Strategy*. New York: McGraw-Hill.
Argyris, C. (1985) *Strategy, Change and Defensive Routines*. London: Pitman.
Argyris, C. and Schon, D.A. (1978) *Organizational Learning: A theory of Action Perspective*. Wokingham: Addison Wesley.
Bartlett, C. and Ghoshal, S. (2002) Building competitive advantage through people. *MIT Sloan Management Review*, 43(2), 34–41.
Boisot, M.H. (1998) *Knowledge Assets: Securing Competitive Advantage in the Information Economy*. Oxford: Open University Press.
Brewer, M.B. (1991) The social self: On being the same and different at the same time. *Personality and Social Psychology Bulletin*, 17, 475–482.
Burns, T. and Stalker, C.M. (1961) *The Management of Innovation*. London: Tavistock.
Burrell, G. and Morgan, G. (1979) *Sociological Paradigms and Organizational Analysis*. London & Exeter: Heinemann.
Byrd, M. and Sparkman, T.E. (2022) Reconciling the business case and the social justice case for diversity: A model of human relations. *Journal of Human Resources Development Review*, 21(1), 75–100. https://doi.org/10.1177/15344843211072356.
Chandler, A.D. (1962) *Strategy and Structure*. Cambridge, MA: MIT Press.
ClickUp. (2023) Available from: ClickUp™ | One app to replace them all.
Combe, C. (2014) *Introduction to Management*. Oxford: Oxford University Press.
Covey, S. (1989) *Seven Habits of Highly Effective People*. New York: Simon & Schuster.
Daft, R.L. and Bensen, A. (2015) *Management*. Hampshire: Annabel Ainscrow for Cengage Learning.
Drucker, P.F. (1946) *Concept of the Corporation*. New York: John Day.
Drucker, P.F. (1974) *Management Tasks, Responsibilities, Practices*. London: Heinemann.
Dyer, W.G. (1986) *Cultural Change in Family Firms*. San Francisco: Jossey-Bass.
Employment Law: Contract. (2023) Available from: www.gov.uk/employment-contracts-and-conditions.
Fayol, H. (1949) *General and Industrial Management* (Translated by Storrs, C.). London: Pitman.
Fries, A., Kammerlander, N. and Leitterstorf, M. (2021) Leadership styles and leadership behaviors in family firms: A systematic literature review. *Journal of Family Business Strategy*, 12(1), 100374. https://doi.org/10.1916/j.jfbs.2020.100374.
Gagliardi, G. and Tzu, S. (2014) *Sun Tzu's The Art of War Plus the Art of Management: Sun Tzu's Strategy for Managers*. Las Vegas: Clearbridge Publishing.

Gilbreth, F.B. and Gilbreth, L.M. (1917) *Applied Motion Study: A Collection of Papers on the Efficient Method to Industrial Preparedness*. New York: Sturgis & Walton. Available from: https://archive.org/details/appliedmotionstu00gilbrich.

Handy, C. (1976) *Understanding Organisations*. London: Penguin.

Handy, C. (1984, 1986) *The Future of Work*. Oxford: Basil Blackwell.

Handy, C. (1988) *The Making of Managers*. London: Longman.

Handy, C. (1990) *The Age of Unreason*. London: Arrow.

Herzberg, F., Mausner, B. and Snyderman, B. (1959) *The Motivation to Work*. New York: Wiley.

Jenson, J. (1989) Different' but not 'exceptional': Canada's Permeable Fordism. *Canadian Review of Sociology and Anthropology*, 26, 69–94.

Nonaka, I. and Takeuchi, H. (1995) *The Knowledge Creating Company: How Japanese Companies Create the Dynamics of Innovation*. Oxford: Oxford University Press.

Levitt, T. (1983) *The Marketing Imagination*. New York: Free Press.

Maslow, A.H. (1970) *Motivation and Personality*. New York: Harper and Row.

Mayo, E.W. (1949) *The Social Problems of an Industrial Civilisation*. London: Routledge and Kegan Paul.

McGregor, D.M. (1960) *The Human Side of Enterprise*. New York: McGraw-Hill.

Mintzberg, H. (1973) *The Nature of Managerial Work*. New York: Harper & Row.

Mintzberg, H. (1989) *Mintzberg on Management*. New York: Free Press.

Nembhard, I.M. and Edmondson, A.C. (2006) Making it safe: The effects of leader inclusiveness and professional status on psychological safety and improvement efforts in health care team. *Journal of Organizational Behaviour*, 27, 941–966.

Ohmae, K. (1982) *The Mind of the Strategist. The Art of Japanese Business*. New York: McGraw-Hill.

Ohmae, K. (1985) *Triad Power: The Coming Shape of Global Competition*. New York: Free Press.

Polyani, M. (1974) *Personal Knowledge: Towards a Post-Critical Philosophy*. Chicago: University of Chicago Press.

Porter, M.E. (1980) *Competitive Strategy: Techniques for Analysing Industries and Competitors*. New York: Free Press.

Schein, E.H. (1985) *Organizational Culture and Leadership*. San Francisco: Jossey-Bass.

Taylor, F.W. (1947) *Principles of Scientific Management*. New York: Harper and Row.

Weber, M. (1930) *The Protestant Ethic and the Spirit of Capitalism*. London: Allen & Unwin.

Witzel, M. (2022) *Management: The Basics*. 2nd Edition. London: Routledge.

## RECOMMENDED FURTHER READING:-

Kennedy, C. (1991) *Guide to the Management Gurus: Shortcuts to the Ideas of Leading Management Thinkers*. London: Business Books.
*Authors' Comment: Kennedy's book is very accessible, and it is easy to follow how management studies have developed.*

Ohame, K. (1990) *The Borderless World: Power and Strategy in the Interlinked Economy*. New York: Harper Business.
*Authors' Comment: This is a classic text on globalisation and it is worth reading in 2023 to see what has manifested and changed in today's world and the significance of Ohmae's foresight.*
Pugh, D.S., Hickson, D.J. and Hinings, C.R. (1983) *Writers on Organisations*. 3rd Edition. Harmondsworth: Penguin.
*Authors' Comment: Very clear and easy to read and an excellent insight into the leading management theorists.*
Witzel, M. (2022) *Management: The Basics*. 2nd Edition. London: Routledge.
*Authors' Comment: An excellent introduction to management.*

## CHAPTER 4

# Careers in marketing

## SYNOPSIS AND LEARNING OUTCOMES

At the end of this chapter, successful students will be able to do the following:

1.  Identify a range of job roles in marketing.
2.  Explain potential career paths in marketing.
3.  Appreciate the opportunities and challenges for marketers building careers in different organisations/scenarios.

As you have read so far, the way marketing is conducted varies from one organisation to another. It also includes many activities, as discussed in Chapter 1. If you are pursuing a career in marketing, you need to consider the different career paths. We'll discuss the key pathways, but you should bear in mind that marketing is changing quickly and it's likely that there will be new roles in the future that we cannot even imagine yet!

We now return to the CIM (2023) definition of *marketing*:

> The management process responsible for identifying, anticipating and satisfying customer requirements profitably.

We will now break this down and think about the roles that may be involved in undertaking marketing. A quick Internet search (April 2023) shows there are many different opportunities in marketing with open vacancies. For example, here are some of the open vacancies at the time of writing:

> Marketing Executive, Head of Marketing, Social Media Executive, Paid Search Specialist, PPC Consultant, Marketing Manager, Senior Marketing Executive, Email Marketing Executive, Digital Marketing Executive, Chief Marketing Officer, Marketing Director Marketing Manager, Marketing Communications Manager, Digital Marketing Manager, Market Research Manager.

DOI: 10.4324/9781003365136-4

The recruitment agency Indeed (2023) identifies ten marketing department roles:

- Marketing manager
- Content creator
- Brand strategist
- Search engine optimisation specialist
- Data analyst
- Public relations manager
- Website developer
- Visual designer
- Ads specialist
- Social media manager

How do you decide what role is best for you? To consider marketing 'in-house' or in an industry setting, you will need to review what part of marketing you enjoy doing and where you want to be.

## IN THE MARKETING INDUSTRY OR IN A MARKETING OCCUPATION?

Another thing you need to consider is whether you want to work in an agency setting or 'in-house', that is, inside an organisation, thus in the marketing and advertising industry or in marketing and advertising occupations across industries. The marketing and advertising industry includes advertising agencies and companies engaged primarily in public relations, communications activities, and media representations. Marketing and advertising occupations across industries include such occupations as marketing, sales, advertising, creative, PR directors, and PR/marketing professionals and advertising account managers.

Many more people work in marketing and advertising occupations, often known as 'in-house' marketing. Marketing professionals who lead marketing will often have an in-house marketing team, but they will also source additional support from the marketing and advertising industry, for example, specialist or full-service agencies. Working in the industry requires many specialist and general skills. There are full-service companies who provide a broad marketing service or specialised agencies that focus on a specific type or sector of marketing. Many agencies' work focuses on aspects of research, such as undertaking research with customers, competitors, and new markets. These agencies will also undertake all the communications involved, which is the full marketing communications mix.

There are also separate agencies for every aspect of marketing, although the majority focus on branding, advertising, digital marketing, design, and public relations. Basically, every aspect of marketing can be covered through agencies in the industry. It is a highly competitive industry, and staff will need to have the right skills, knowledge, and attributes to succeed. Much of the work in agencies will be negotiating and communicating with business-to-business customers and then helping your customers undertake marketing to their customers. These roles, for example, may include account directors, account managers, design and creative directors, and media buying executives.

## WHAT YOU ENJOY DOING AND WHERE YOU WANT TO BE

**FIGURE 4.19** Digital marketing image.

We can see that marketing can have a science-type activity and a creative-type activity. Are you interested in finding out how and why things work? Analysing information to create market intelligence? If so, something in market research, intelligence, coding, or planning could be ideal for you. It's not just that, though – how about new product development and creating and developing innovations? There is lots of opportunities here for scientists, developers, and researchers. If you're creative, perhaps you like designing or creating content. A lot of marketing activity relies on creative approaches. A strong creative campaign can include many different activities across public relations (PR), advertising, and social media. Someone must come up with the idea and turn it into a planned campaign that reaches the target market. This is where integrated marketing communications comes into play! Alongside this, there is a need to plan, direct, manage, and budget. Do you want to direct and manage others? If so, perhaps you may need to think about how you might progress to a marketing manager/director type of role. You can progress through the ranks, of course, but you will need to develop skills along the way. Many university graduates progress quickly up the ranks in marketing, particularly if they are digitally minded and willing to work anywhere in the world.

The growth in digital marketing offers a vast range of opportunities over and above the traditional marketing role. There is also the added complication of artificial intelligence, such as ChatGPT, and what this means for marketers (as well as other roles, of course). It is likely that we still do not yet know what impact this will have on the industry, but technological developments are likely to have a huge impact on roles within marketing. For her professional doctoral studies, Dixon-Todd (2019) undertook research with academics and practitioners working in marketing; the issues they presented are applicable at the current time. Highlights in relation to job roles included the following insights:

Finding graduates with the right skills set is also a challenge.

Practitioners state that disciplines merge and the fluidity of disciplines seemed to be less of an issue, and they may be a member of more than one professional body, work between disciplines or manage across disciplines depending on the needs of the business/client.

Some practitioners utilised specialist agencies with a focus on sector rather than communications discipline.

There is acknowledgement that the industry is changing, and agencies and individuals are expected to change with it.

Just keeping up with the changes is a challenge. Technology and the digital transformation mean practitioners are having to work differently and that new roles have been created.

There are many different communications disciplines crossing over one another and that such communications roles now undertake wider marketing and management tasks.

The industry is merging; clients and companies want more return on investment and there is a greater need for data driven marketing.

Thus, it can be seen that whichever role you set out to achieve, you can expect fluidity, change, and the need for lifelong learning! The practicalities of working in marketing and the requirement to adapt to change are presented in the examples of the following case studies.

## CASE STUDY 4.1

*Dr Yvonne Dixon-Todd*

### Insight into a marketing career

I obtained my first 'proper' job – a one-year placement through university – as marketing assistant at a public transport company. This was a fantastic time in my life. An opportunity to put theory into practice and see things happen really quickly. At that time, I was working in a subsidiary of the main group, and I was part of a small team reporting to the marketing manager, with plenty of opportunity to make a difference. My work centred on marketing communications, and I assisted with direct marketing, advertising (posters and local radio), internal marketing, community relations, and market research. I really did learn a considerable amount during my placement year, and I am forever grateful to the University of Sunderland for giving me the opportunity. Towards the end of my placement, I was appointed to the post of marketing officer, and then to a centralised position as marketing manager north, and then again promoted to overall marketing manager. I rose rapidly in the organisation – taking on more responsibility. I was responsible for:

- Identifying opportunities for business growth and development and implementing initiatives to maximise revenue.
- Maintaining good relationships with key business and political stakeholders.
- Networking through the Chamber of Commerce, the Bridge Club, the Chartered Institute of Management, etc. to encourage positive support for transport initiatives.
- Writing the marketing plan for inclusion in the corporate plan, and then managing the implementation of it through a team of staff.
- Managing and leading the operations of a broad range of marketing functions – marketing research, marketing communications, customer services, travel centres.
- Line management of over 20 staff.
- Managing a significant budget and outsourcing design, print, website development, advertising and media buying, marketing research, and PR.

Reflecting back on this time, I look back to it with real fondness. I found my love of marketing, of learning and doing, and of making a difference to my organisation and to my career. It was a real foundation for the work I have undertaken in later life, educating and supporting the marketers of tomorrow.

If you are interested in working in marketing, it is advisable to explore the Chartered Institute of Marketing. The CIM is the professional body that offers a range of qualifications, short courses, memberships, and the chartered marketer status. Many marketing and business degrees in the UK offer dual accreditation, which means students can obtain a professional qualification and a degree.

In the following section, Dr Yvonne Dixon-Todd shares her personal journey with the Chartered Institute of Marketing.

I first became involved with the Chartered Institute of Marketing (CIM) as a student, whilst studying for my degree at the University of Sunderland. A lecturer at that time advised that those studying BA business studies with a marketing specialisation could obtain some exemptions from the CIM qualifications. Once out on placement as a marketing assistant, I completed the postgraduate diploma from the CIM, and I have been a member ever since. I even taught on the CIM programmes and became an examiner on their marketing communications module. The next step was to become the CIM student contact on the North-East local committee. Following several years, I was promoted to vice chair of the North-East committee, and following a reorganisation within CIM, I accepted a position on their Regional North-East Board. Again, this position focused on the marketing education aspect. In 2015, I became a member of the CIM Learning Advisory Group, now called the CIM Experts List (on a voluntary basis), and therefore resigned from the North-East Committee. I do, however, still have close links with the Committee and remain committed to developing marketing and marketing education within the North-East. Reflecting on my time with the CIM, I can see that each of the roles that I have undertaken with them has been broadly in line with my current full-time role at any given time. For instance, as I have become more strategic in my full-time role, so too has my role within CIM. I have fully engaged with the professional body and am now a fellow. I envisage being a FCIM for life. I recommend that you take the time to explore CIM (2023).

Dr Andrew Kristoffer Dean has worked in a number of different roles and offers his personal insights into marketing next.

## CASE STUDY 4.2
*Dr Andrew Kristoffer Dean*

### Marketing in science technology: 'magic' – becoming the scientist seller

For many of us, scientists are those curious laboratory 'boffins' who spend their days trying to understand the secrets of the universe, usually while pondering on complex theorems and wearing white coats and safety spectacles. With such popular tropes tending to depict scientists as the arbiters of lasers, chemicals, and things that go bang, it is hardly surprising that they are frequently mythologised as modern-day sorcerers and praised for ushering in a utopianist high-technology future. Although this enchanting narrative helps populate laboratories with individuals keen to save the world, there are, of course, scientists working outside of the laboratory, particularly in commercial science. With little attention having been paid to this arena,

I will now draw on over a decade's worth of my experiences as a scientist seller and tell a brief tale of a different type of science, related to sales. So let us start with the most obvious question: What exactly is a *scientist seller*? Not surprisingly, and as the name suggests, it is an individual trained in science who subsequently sells scientific products/services to the public or other businesses.

When we consider the high social regard given to laboratory scientists, we might wonder why anyone would try to turn their hands to sales, particularly when sellers and marketers are frequently framed as silver-tongued. Yet there are a myriad of perfectly good reasons for moving out of the laboratory and changing career, including a lack of laboratory jobs, long hours every week, aggressive cultures requiring continuous innovative output, and dubious job security. While scientific sales can also have some of these problems, there tend to be vacancies, opportunities for rapid career advancement, chances for international travel, and high financial rewards for those who can thrive in the commercial world. Problematically, though, with scientists typically being trained exclusively in biology, chemistry, and physics, there is often a poverty of understanding about marketing, which can create ongoing sales tensions, even for the most committed individual. Unfortunately, this issue is compounded by most scientific companies wrongly believing that high-technology products will simply sell themselves. As this is seldom the case, scientists can be left struggling to market their products and services and, even worse, failing to make the sale. Consequently, new scientist sellers often spend their days asking, 'How do I sell this?' 'How do I explain a product that nobody has heard of?' and 'How do I sell to people who aren't scientists?' Condensing these questions, scientist sellers must cultivate key marketing skills to explain what products are and how they work to diverse professional audiences.

While I might be tempted to argue that the solution is for scientist sellers to embrace sociolinguistics and cognitive psychology, there are, of course, simpler and more pragmatic ways to achieve success in high-technology sales endeavours. In other words, if the solution is more complex than the problem, it should probably be ignored. As such, my first recommendation is for scientists to break out of the mindset of just being the 'scientist' and accept that a scientist seller is a hybrid identity, requiring new skills in communication, particularly towards disseminating product information to different groups of people. Discursively, this might include using metaphors, product simplification, or even linking products to popular science fiction movies and books. What matters most is developing close relationships with potential buyers and building on what other individuals already know while supporting them to develop new technical product knowledge. Furthermore, there is an acute need for scientists to allow themselves to embrace a life outside of mainstream science and recognise that without scientific sales, there would be no discoveries, no innovation, and ultimately, no science.

Finally, while scientist sellers can easily find themselves isolated from more traditional marketing, this need not be the case. There is no reason to 'go it alone'. This is particularly the case when we consider the ever-growing number of marketing trade bodies and organisations offering training, qualifications, and support in technical communications. Also, with online learning, we are entering a new era for flexible learning and the ability to access global experts, even in niche areas. As such, I believe there has never been a better time to consider a career in commercial science and to be involved in taking products to market. The only real challenge for any scientist is to imagine a future of multiple professional possibilities, where selling can be just as important as being in a laboratory. As such, this more unusual professional pathway is not an abandonment of science but rather a new way of being a scientist and wearing a less-traditional coat.

The following suggestions may help support the start of your professional identity, which is further discussed in Chapter 6.

Mr Benjamin Spence gives his recommendations for marketers starting out:

> I recommend starting to build a portfolio as soon as you can, either digitally, as hard copies, or a combination of both. Any tasks completed, no matter the size, should be added to this on a regular basis. When opportunities arise to discuss what you have done to date, this complements the conversation with visual aspects, where you can 'show off' your skills and experiences.
>
> Make the effort to attend networking events; however, try to aim for quality over quantity with these. Spend the time and effort to attend events where you are most likely to meet peers which will provide personal and business opportunities. It's not all about getting thousands of connections on LinkedIn; just make sure you have a 'snazzy' business card at the ready once these initial connections are established. From a personal experience, when starting out, this led to not only several successful marketing opportunities but also the formation of relationships with experienced marketeers who became personal friends and mentors.

And Dr Andrew Kristoffer Dean's tips for starting out: 'Embrace the natural sciences, explore pharmacology, neuroscience, and genetics. The answers to our questions about marketing exist within ourselves, at the atomic level and above.'

## WANT TO GAIN EXPERIENCE?

So how might you learn more about what it is like to work in marketing? Look for opportunities to gain work experience, such as internships, placements, work-based assignments, or student competitions. A great example of this is, in 2023, the MA marketing students at the University of Sunderland won the Greggs Marketing Challenge. Here's an insight into this experience.

### The Greggs Marketing Challenge – what's it all about?

Read the following press release to find out more.

#### _A proper taste of success_

A team of postgraduate students from our business school tasted success after winning a prestigious regional marketing competition with their recommendation of a new 'proper' range for leading food on the go retailer Greggs.

The Greggs Marketing Challenge is an annual event hotly contested by student teams from four of the North-East regional universities.

This year, students were invited to present a 20-minute pitch based on the brief 'Embracing diversity across the business: how can Greggs' products best represent the communities that they serve?' and including a maximum of three new products.

The Sunderland team's proposal was to introduce a groundbreaking range of food items incorporating flavours from popular and upcoming cuisine trends, designed to not exclude customers on belief, diet, or price. The range – an Indian keema bake, North African salad, and Persian chicken wrap – stays true to Greggs' current product offering but replaces meat with Halal-certified Quorn, thus making it acceptable to vegetarians, vegans, and those whose diet is shaped by religious beliefs.

The team called the range 'Greggs Proper', with the word 'proper' chosen because of its associations of being correct, accepted, kosher, and as a word often used to describe halal products. It is also a nod to Greggs' Northern heritage; _proper_ is a colloquial term used throughout the North-East.

In addition to the proposed food range, the team suggested a number of Greggs stores be converted into 'proper' stores. These would stock the new range plus all

**FIGURE 4.20** Students winning Greggs: C. Southern, O. Akingbo, O. Owolabi, and C. Moore.

Greggs' current vegetarian and vegan products, drinks, cakes, sandwiches, fries, crisps, etc., but no meat products. The recommendation was for such stores to be strategically selected based on population demographics and be supplied by regional ghost kitchens which would create the vegan, vegetation, kosher, and halal ranges to avoid any cross-contamination.

A comparative pricing strategy was also recommended to avoid discrimination on price, and a proposed multimedia promotional campaign included the use of community spaces, food vans at events and festivals, and even specific micro-social media influencers to help spread the word. Speaking about the event, university team coach Kris Woods said:

> The students worked hard on their presentation and the results were visible for all to see; they came up with a truly transformational proposal which went to the heart of the brief. I am extremely proud of their work ethic, their achievement, and their performance, which was exemplary.

Teams from Newcastle, Teesside, and Northumbria Universities also participated in the event, and there was an agonizing 40-minute wait while the judges deliberated and the winner was announced. Sunderland was highly commended for the breadth of their research and for delivering a well-thought-out presentation that considered diversity and inclusivity across all elements of the business.

## Task 4.1

As you're reading this book, we presume you'd like a job in 'marketing'. But doing what? Take ten minutes to note down the answer to the following: What would your dream job entail? What type of organisation would you like to work for? Or would you set up your own business? And if so, doing what?

## Task 4.2

Make two lists (1) of science-related marketing roles and (2) of art-related roles.

## Task 4.3

Read the Greggs case study. Where do you think marketing is evident? What type of tasks were undertaken by the team?

## SUMMARY OF CHAPTER 4

In this chapter we have provided some insight into careers in marketing. There is so much change in this field that one thing is certain: there will always be many opportunities and challenges. You might want to work in the marketing industry or in a marketing occupation. Many more people decide to work in a marketing occupation role. When developing a career path, you need to consider what type of role you might like and what matches your skill set and attributes.

## REFERENCES

CIM. (2023) *What Is Marketing*. Available from: 7ps.pdf (cim.co.uk) (Accessed 22 April 2023).

Dixon-Todd, Y. (2019) *Enhancing the Teaching of Marketing in Higher Education: An Integrated Marketing Communications Perspective*. Professional Doctorate, University of Sunderland. Unpublished.

Indeed. (2023) *Marketing Roles*. Available from: Job Search | Indeed Marketing Roles Jobs – 2023 | Indeed.com (Accessed 22 April 2023).

CHAPTER 5

# The skills and knowledge needed in marketing

SYNOPSIS AND LEARNING OUTCOMES

At the end of this chapter, successful students will be able to do the following:

1. Review job descriptions and identify the key skills and knowledge needed in different marketing roles.
2. Demonstrate an appreciation of the importance of soft and hard skills.
3. Explain key marketing knowledge that is most often applied in practical settings.

## INTRODUCTION

Once you have considered a potential career in marketing, it is then time to explore different roles in more depth. Let's think about the skills and knowledge needed to be a success. Do you need a degree to be successful? Not necessarily; however, it is expected that you will have the necessary skills and knowledge and a growth mindset. Therefore, be willing to try new things and learn and develop, regardless of age or position.

This chapter explores academic and practitioner viewpoints on the skills and knowledge needed. It also provides some example job descriptions; however, please just search and see what you can find – there are many real-life examples, of course.

## WHAT DOES A DEGREE GIVE YOU?

When considering a degree, it is necessary to think about what employability skills, both generic and disciplinary, and attributes are included in such an award (National Careers Service, 2023). The emphasis on students developing practical knowledge and skills that can be transferred from an educational setting to the workplace has gained dominance

DOI: 10.4324/9781003365136-5

in the policy discourse on the role of higher education. When degrees are written, they are designed to meet a number of professional standards and regulatory body requirements that are relevant to marketing, for instance, the QAA (Quality Assurance Agency for Higher Education), Chartered Institute of Marketing, Chartered Institute of Public Relations, and Institute of Practitioners in Advertising.

The QAA benchmark statements (2023) show the requirement that 'graduates need to develop strong writing skills, managerial abilities, graphic design, and knowledge of persuasion and marketing'. While there are specialist skills in different subject areas, in general terms, these employment skills are accepted to be the skills of self-management, communications, numeracy, use of IT, and teamworking (Career Skills and Training, 2023). Intertwined in the different opinions of what the skills content of the higher education curriculum should contain are the varying perspectives of how much these skills should centre on vocational education and training. These two perspectives are also affected by whether the subject is viewed as scientifically or art based.

## WHAT DOES A PROFESSIONAL BODY GIVE YOU?

Professional bodies provide a wealth of information and networking opportunities as well as development courses and approved professional qualifications. They also provide recognition that can differentiate you when applying for roles. In previous chapters, marketers and academics shared their insights, and in Chapter 1, Veronica Swindale talked about the Northeast Sales and Marketing Academy, which offers a range of professional body courses and awards. Here, Kris Woods provides an insight into her work with the Chartered Institute of Marketing (CIM):

> The world of marketing is constantly changing; indeed, it has changed significantly since my early days, which is why I am a staunch advocate of continuous professional development and ongoing learning. It is what enables me to remain relevant in an increasingly digital world. An integral element of my own CPD was the achievement of the CIM professional diploma in marketing, an applied learning programme which required the assimilation of my practical skills and experience with the academic tools and models of marketing. As a result, I have a multifaceted approach to marketing, which has helped me deliver successful marketing programmes in industry and, more recently, in the classroom.

We would recommend exploring the various professional organisations. For example, extracts from the websites of professional bodies are noted here:

> The CIM (2023) has supported the marketing sector. With over 20,000 members in more than 100 countries, CIM strives for business leaders and opinion formers to recognise the positive contribution professional marketing can bring to their

organisations, the economy and wider society. We support, develop and represent marketers, organisations and the profession all over the world. Our ability to award Chartered Marketer status recognises a marketer's commitment to staying current and abiding by a professional Code of Conduct. While our diverse range of training courses and world-renowned qualifications enable modern marketers to thrive in their roles and deliver long-term success for businesses.

The Chartered Institute of Public Relations (CIPR) is 'the world's only Royal Chartered professional body for public relations practitioners, with nearly 10,000 members'. The CIPR (2023) states:

> Our members are recognised PR professionals. We work with and for them to set, maintain and advance standards. We do this through our industry respected qualifications; our Continuing Professional Development scheme, Accreditation and Chartership programmes; our open, in-house and bespoke training; our industry awards and conferences; and the production of research, best practice and skills guidance.

The Data and Marketing Association (2023) states that it is

> the driving force of intelligent marketing. . . . Guided by our customer-first principles enshrined in the DMA Code, we champion a rich fusion of technology, diverse talent, creativity, research and insight to set standards for the UK's data and marketing community to meet in order to thrive. . . . Through DMA Talent we create pathways for the next generation of marketers to emerge; our world-class training institute, the Institute of Data & Marketing (IDM) delivers learning at corporate and individual levels, championing micro-upskilling; and through the DMA we deliver advocacy, legal and compliance support, research, insight and a packed events calendar.

The Institute of Advertising Practitioners (2023) advise that:

> Every year we help more than 4,000 practitioners future-proof their careers through our Continuous Professional Development Programme. We don't just keep their careers on track, we help them flourish. We set the protocols for the UK industry's best practice standards. So, we can advise on how to choose an agency or how to run an agency. We also work collaboratively with our members to achieve our goal to improve diversity within the industry. We listen to agency issues so that we can set or update policy or lead the industry response on whatever might be troubling them.

There are, of course, many other professional bodies, and you should search for them and find one that is suitable for you. In addition to utilising professional body materials, you can read practitioner magazines, such as *Marketing Week*, *Campaign*, *Brand Republic*, and *The Drum*, as well as the many online newsletters, websites, and industry competitions.

**FIGURE 5.21** Marketing meeting around a table.

Now, let's think specifically about roles in marketing.

When considering the skills required by those working in marketing, practitioners recognise the need for staff to be able to work across disciplines, that integration requires both specialised expert and generalist skills, but also that few people can do this, as many have only worked in traditional single-discipline areas. Many skills are identified by practitioners, including leadership, diplomacy, creativity, analytics, coordination, and ability to see the bigger picture. Characteristics are also required, including 'inquisitiveness, a lack of ego and self-confidence', and 'successful IMC professionals need to have five critical skills that include alignment with organisational goals, setting measurable goals, high level thinking, coordination capabilities and mastery of all communications tools' (Dixon-Todd, 2019). Therefore, it can be seen that there is consensus in the practitioner research field about the need for specialist and generalists in this field, which creates a conundrum for the educator.

Dixon-Todd and Hall (2018, p. 3) also identify that a skills gap currently exists:

> Practitioners identify that those undertaking IMC tend to be in more senior roles and that there is a skills shortage at the middle level – those that understand both old and new media; There are now roles that have never previously been needed and this is causing a skills gap; Recruitment of graduates with qualifications and good work experience is difficult.

Mr Benjamin Spence provides his insights into the skills needed by marketers:

*Creative skills*. How can you promote your initiative that will differentiate from competitors and simultaneously resonate with consumers? Think outside the box, off-the-wall marketing!

*Interpersonal skills*. Whether you are working with an external partner, leading a team of marketeers, or pitching to the marketing director, you need the ability to adapt your style and approach, mindful of other personalities, in order to achieve the most return on the initiative.

*Digital skills*. Not just trends and TikToks, but marketers need to be aware of digital touch points within your customer journey mapping. If you're not there, your competitors will be. If your competitors are there, how can you approach this space differently and more effectively?

## IN PRACTICE

We will now consider three different roles: digital marketing executive, senior account manager, and head of marketing.

## EXAMPLE 1

### Digital marketing executive

This role will have you working in a close-knit company where learning and development are key to what they do. You'll be alongside the marketing manager, who will help you develop skills in the more organic side of digital marketing. Complimenting their skill set, you'll be using your knowledge in paid ads and SEO to drive campaigns across a number of platforms to success, platforms such as Google, Bing, Facebook, and Spotify.

The type of person they are looking for is naturally creative, with a passion for both marketing and gaming. Your combined passions will allow you to speak to the target audiences in a way they will understand, since you would be a part of that group. Beyond your passions and creativity, curiosity in how to improve your campaigns will be a big bonus.

### *Key skills*

- 2 years' experience in paid ads.
- Experience with Google Search, Google Performance Max, and Google Analytics.
- Exceptional copywriting, editing, and proofreading skills.
- Understand how to best manage budgets across multiple channels.
- Great communication skills across multiple departments.

## Key responsibilities

- Regularly monitor paid channels across platforms like Google, Facebook, and Spotify.
- Conduct audits and identify ways to optimise productivity and efficiency.
- Conduct keyword research in an effort to improve SEO.
- Keep up to date with both channel and market trends.

# EXAMPLE 2

## Senior account manager

### Purpose

To deliver excellent performance across every aspect of our client work, ensuring that relevant client strategies are set up and successfully delivered to achieve client goals.

With the role working in a highly supportive and award-winning team handling campaigns for some of the region's leading brands, you can expect to work on a range of campaign activities that span media relations, content creation, social media, influencer outreach, events, brand development, and marketing communications.

### Responsibilities

You will be working closely with senior members of the team to plan and deliver client campaigns and projects. As a key person in a small team, you will regularly have to cover both strategic and operational functions on the planning and delivery of client work. The main responsibilities of this role are set out next.

### Developing excellent relationships with client teams/understanding client businesses

- Forming a deep understanding of the issues affecting our clients' businesses and the sectors in which they operate so that you are able to produce relevant campaign ideas, make sound decisions, and give good quality advice and responses to typical client requirements.

### Producing effective work that achieves client goals

- Ensuring you deliver effectively against client campaign goals.
- Writing of media releases and content for social media, website/blogs, and print materials that engage and inform.
- Achieving our commercial targets.
- You will play an active part, through a mixture or pitching, proposal writing, networking, and cross-selling our service lines with new and existing clients, to help us meet our own commercial objectives.

### *Coaching and mentoring junior team (where relevant)*

- Assisting any junior team members to continue to develop their skills in their role supporting the work you are leading.
- Taking the time to explain or show 'how to' where relevant.
- Identifying any professional development you think is required.

### *Key skills*

- Excellent experience of planning and delivering PR/integrated campaigns that align with client goals.
- Excellent project management capabilities.
- Able to think ahead to see any issues arising for clients or self so that these can be avoided/handled effectively.
- Confidence in personal decision-making.
- Creative thinker and solution-finder.

### *Key traits*

- Takes full responsibility for work under your control.
- An excellent team player who can work well with others and thrives on collaboration and seeing everyone in the team succeed.
- Willing and wanting to continue to learn new skills.
- Has curiosity to know more about the work we do, the clients we work with.
- Works with intellectual rigour to be confident in defending own/team ideas with conviction.
- Respectfully challenges things where relevant to do so to get better results or outcomes.
- Is willing to manage difficult situations with integrity.
- Resilient, upbeat, and professional.
- Confident in dealing with board-level members of client teams/running high-level meetings and strategy workshops.

### *Knowledge/professional interests*

- Good understanding of the general business and news landscape of the North-East.
- Good understanding of the national news and business landscape.
- Willing to get under the skin of the issues affecting/surrounding client sectors.

## EXAMPLE 3

## Head of marketing

A superb opportunity to join a very successful SME business with a creative, positive, and growth-oriented culture. This growing company is keen to invest in its marketing team and seeks a head of marketing to work closely with the MD to drive the business forward and oversee the finance function. A business that truly cares about its people and is keen to promote from within, this position presents a great opportunity for career development.

The head of marketing will lead the marketing team and develop and execute effective marketing strategies. As head of marketing, you will be responsible for developing and implementing marketing plans that will increase brand awareness, drive customer engagement, and generate sales growth. You will also be responsible for overseeing the execution of all marketing campaigns, analysing performance metrics, and identifying areas for improvement.

## Principal activities

- Develop and implement strategic marketing plans that align with business goals.
- Lead, coach, and develop the marketing team, ensuring that goals and objectives are met.
- Manage the company's branding, messaging, and positioning in the market.
- Develop and implement multi-channel marketing campaigns to drive lead generation, customer acquisition and retention, and revenue growth.
- Collaborate with cross-functional teams, including sales, product, and customer operations, to ensure alignment and maximise the impact of marketing programs.
- Conduct market research and analysis to identify trends, opportunities, and customer needs.
- Monitor and report on the effectiveness of marketing campaigns and make recommendations for improvement.
- Manage marketing budgets and allocate resources effectively to maximise ROI.
- Stay up to date with the latest marketing trends, technologies, and best practices.

## Qualifications and experience

- Bachelor's degree in marketing or related field; master's degree preferred.
- 7+ years of experience in marketing, with at least 3 years in a leadership role.
- Demonstrated ability to develop and implement successful marketing campaigns.
- Experience with a variety of marketing channels, including digital, social, email, events, and content marketing.
- Strong analytical and data-driven decision-making skills.
- Ability to work collaboratively with cross-functional teams.
- Strong project management skills and ability to prioritise and manage multiple projects simultaneously.

As you can see, three very different jobs, but all under the remit of marketing. Try the tasks at the end of this chapter to draw out the synergies between the three roles.

The skills and knowledge required for these roles were acknowledged in the research by Dixon-Todd (2019). The following are extracts from the practitioners.

When interviewing the associate director of a professional body, it was clear they appreciated the benefit of education and practice when they said that '[e]ducation and practical skills from work experience is what is needed . . . and we need for someone to understand what works but also why it works – theory can help here'.

The owner of the marketing consultancy agreed that having the education enhanced the practices of those working in marketing. They said that '[t]here needs to be academic knowledge, you need to know what the rules are before you can break them but can say how and why'. They also recognised that technology has changed things but the foundations still need to be there.

> New staff just think new media and forget about the old but also traditional media knowledge is declining. . . . Technology, adapting to technology. Understanding the benefits but also the harm that can be done. And the belief that technology is 'free' and doesn't need to be managed. Digital, but we're still using the traditional media to signpost the new digital. Understanding markets and the Twitter generation.

The owner of a communications recruitment agency identified the following issues for marketing and communications roles:

> More people are doing more content. You are no longer specialist but trying to be everything, and I think a lot of people are having to reinvent themselves. . . . The way people consume media is changing. So the breadth of expertise is needed. . . . Need good work experience, strong writing skills.

Other frequent responses linked to having the right qualifications, being a member of a professional body (the owner of a PR company said 'I am a fellow of the CIPR and the CIM'), having confidence in being able to adapt, mix, and create chemistry. General skills, such as collaboration, teamwork, communication, and time management, also came up. The CEO of a marketing consultancy and the chair of a professional body provided an extensive list for applicants to consider:

> Communications, storytelling, curiosity, passion and drive, reliable and accountable, some self-doubt, open to change, adaptable, take constructive criticism, purposeful, problem solver, good with numbers, shared values, and experiences.

The feedback from the practitioner participants is extensive and demonstrates the breadth of skills and characteristics required by someone to successfully progress in a career in marketing.

Let's go back to the question of whether you need a degree to be successful. Hopefully, by reviewing this chapter, you can see that a qualification, be that a degree or a professional qualification, can help you demonstrate you have the skills and knowledge. Having a qualification sets you apart from lots of the competition, and it is something that can never be taken away from you. Dr Dixon-Todd discusses her approach to qualifications:

> I undertook a degree in business studies (with a marketing specialism) and then took professional qualifications from the CIM, the Chartered Institute of Public Relations, and the Market Research Society whilst working. I decided to focus on marketing planning and marketing communications and specialised in these for my MA marketing and doctoral study.

# TASKS

## Task 5.1

This task invites you to work on your graduate skills of communications, report writing, and numeracy (Career Skills and Training, 2023).
**Vegetarian shop and café – costing the launch**

Look back to the project management for the launch of the new vegetarian shop and café (Chapter 3). In the project management task, in Chapter 3, you were invited to consider the budget and how you would allocate funds to each part of the planned launch.

For this task, go back to the budget and refine the spending and work out the calculations in detail. Start with how much you allocated in the planning of the launch, and present the details in a formal report format.

## Task 5.2

Read the jobs and quotes from participants and identify the different skills required.

## Task 5.3

Read the chapter and look at other job roles and what key areas of marketing knowledge are required.

# SUMMARY OF CHAPTER 5

In this chapter we have presented the more practical side of marketing through consideration of the skills and knowledge needed in marketing roles. Marketing roles demand high-level skills in self-management, communications, numeracy, use of IT, and teamworking, amongst others. It is important to take every opportunity to develop a deep understanding of the complexity of the interactions across and between the various facets of marketing but have the knowledge and skills to manage tactical strategies within the different sectors.

# REFERENCES

Career Skills and Training. (2023) Available from: Career skills and training – GOV.UK (www.gov.uk) (Accessed 1 May 2023).

CIM. (2023) *CIM Careers*. Available from: (cim-careers.co.uk) (Accessed 1 May 2023).

CIPR. (2023) About Us. Available from: (cipr.co.uk) (Accessed 1 May 2023).

Dixon-Todd, Y. (2019) *Enhancing the Teaching of Marketing in Higher Education: An Integrated Marketing Communications Perspective*. Professional Doctorate, University of Sunderland. Unpublished.

Dixon-Todd, Y. and Hall, L. (2018) The state of integrated marketing communications education: Insights from industry – but do we all agree? Academy of Marketing Conference Proceedings.

DMA. (2023) *About the DMA* (Accessed 1 May 2023).
National Careers Service. (2023) Available form: The Skills Toolkit | National Careers Service (Accessed 1 May 2023).
QAA. (2023) *Benchmark Statements*. Available from: Subject Benchmark Statement – Business and Management (qaa.ac.uk) (Accessed 1 May 2023).

## RECOMMENDED FURTHER READING

Career Skills and Training. (2023) Available from: Career skills and training – GOV.UK (www.gov.uk) (Accessed 1 May 2023).
CIM. (2023) *CIM Careers*. Available from: (cim-careers.co.uk) (Accessed 1 May 2023).
*Authors' comments: The above two websites provide extensive guidance on developing skills and offer information on valuable training opportunities.*

## CHAPTER 6

# Professional identity in business and in marketing

## SYNOPSIS AND LEARNING OUTCOMES

At the end of this chapter, successful students will be able to do the following:

1. Explain the core concepts of professional identity.
2. Apply the concepts of professional identity to their own situation.
3. Identify and plan for roles in their preferred area of marketing and preferred industry.

## INTRODUCTION

This chapter explores how professional identity is developed in different professions and in marketing. In this chapter, the nature of professional identity will be examined. In marketing, as in other professions, professional identity is self-realisation and how you present yourself within your own profession. It is built up over time and includes how you view yourself and how you interact with others within a professional situation. It is a complex mix of influences from your life experience and interactions with others. In most professions, it can be seen as the 'image of the professional' in that area, and in marketing, it can be defined as your personal brand. We discuss personal profiles and statements in the next chapter, and here we introduce to you how you can develop your 'brand identity'. It is important as a business professional to be authentic, and as presented by management theorists in Chapter 3, business professionals must ensure they can work effectively across different parts of the business sectors (Barkas and Armstrong, 2021; Barkas et al., 2021). In terms of the management theorists we have presented in previous chapters, they are their own 'brand ambassadors' of their work.

In his research, Scott (2008, p. 219) explored how professional people are both created and defined by the professions they work in. So learning how to create your own identity/

DOI: 10.4324/9781003365136-6

brand is as much a part of working within the boundaries of the profession as it is about presenting your own image within it. He said that:

> Our conception of professionals, as is true of all social phenomena, is shaped by two distinctive, but interrelated factors. It is influenced, first, by changes in the structure and composition of those occupations that we identify by this label; and second, it is affected by changes in the theoretical lenses we bring to bear in examining these occupations.
>
> (Scott, 2008, p. 220)

So as important as it is to form a professional identity, it is equally important to learn what is expected within that profession. Scott's (2008) research into professional identity examined how early studies in the 1930s to 1960s were based on professions such as law and medicine and revealed the expectations of behaviour/identity were functionalist in approach based on formal knowledge and were practice-based. However, a conflict theory of professionalisation began to emerge from the 1960s during a period of anti-war protests; there began an alternative conflict thesis whereby the privileged position of professionals was challenged through research that explored the nature of professional power in a shift of analysis, as summarised by Morgan and Quack (2006, p. 406, quoted in Scott, 2008, p. 221):

> In effect, the nature of professional power is a reflection of the way in which the state relates to social groups within it: is the predominant mode of state engagement toward structuring and shaping social groups or is the state itself an outcome of the actions of social groups and not dependent or 'superior' to it?

In response to the aforementioned tensions, Scott (2008) developed a broad framework for the study of organisations based on his argument that '[i]nstitutions are comprised of regulative, normative, and cultural-cognitive elements that, together with associated activities and resources, provide stability and meaning to social life' (2008, p. 48). While he stressed that the institutional elements are symbolic in nature, they do impact on social behaviour. The rules, norms, and beliefs are regulative, normative, and cognitive, and it is their interface and interaction that form the professional identity of the organisation.

During the recent Covid-19 pandemic, many professions, and the medical profession in particular, were forced to review their professional identity around patient care. This was because the immediacy of the response required by the pandemic necessitated, more than ever, the requirement to evolve and work across multi-disciplinary teams. The pressure was, therefore, placed on the medical and related professions to adapt from within the organisation. This situation stressed the importance for the need for changing roles, the importance of clear communications and the principles that underpin effective teamworking, and the critical importance of inclusive practice (Kamara and Moulds, 2020).

The following case study provides an insight into how self-awareness can help formulate professional identity.

## CASE STUDY 6.1
*Dr Ian Carr*

Dr Ian Carr worked in various leadership roles in the banking sector for 25 years before moving into higher education in 2005. In his current role at the University of Sunderland, Ian works closely with leaders from a variety of businesses, from SMEs to large corporate organisations in the public and private sectors, supporting the development of leadership and management skills. He has found that understanding professional identity is a key element in career development, and this is achieved through increasing self-awareness, the foundation of personal and professional effectiveness.

What Dr Carr's research and experience indicate is that appropriate support and challenge, underpinned by feedback and reflection, increase self-awareness, enhance confidence, and clarify aspirations, influencing individual authenticity and perceptions of employability.

**FIGURE 6.22** Image of professional identity.

The ways in which self-awareness is achieved or increased are identified as through challenging experience and what is perceived to be the significance of the challenge. It is clear that challenging experience creates genuine self-awareness and self-belief, which cannot be achieved through observation or feedback alone, and that heightened awareness is most likely to be achieved through post-experience reflection. In terms of professional development, self-knowledge or self-awareness is considered to be a key concern. Self-awareness relates to having a deep understanding of personal strengths and weaknesses, learned preferences, and insight into one's impact on others in interpersonal contexts.

It is evident from Dr Carr's research that experience has a considerable effect upon individual understanding of ways of thinking and acting, that challenge transforms personality, and that experience is important in forming character. Clarity of career aspirations comes from increased awareness, including realisation of purpose, becoming more motivated and aspirational, and understanding that an individual does not have to settle for something that they do not want. The factors that influence and promote the transformation of awareness are challenge, support, feedback, and reflection.

### Challenge

Challenge is strongly equated with assertiveness of identity. Reflection appears to be particularly influential upon the extent of an individual's transformation, notably the benefits of stepping outside of the experience, the value of looking back over a timeline, away from the pressures of a role and an organisation, creating a realisation of what an individual has been through, and how far they have come, how much they have grown.

Understanding values is particularly beneficial in this process of becoming; challenge appears to raise awareness of values, with reflection being the vehicle to become conscious of those values, to be sensitive to their impact upon emotions and behaviour, and to make sense of experiences in order to make significant decisions.

## Confidence

Confidence is often experienced as evolutionary, reported to take an initial dip when challenge 'kicks in', but with support, the overall transition is reported to be a positive one. In such circumstances, overall growth in confidence is reported to be substantial, sustained, and transforming, becoming *'locked into'* the individual being, rather than superficial and temporary. This does not mean that self-doubt is eliminated, but working through and coping with challenge builds resilience to future challenge and a disposition to cope with future doubt.

Sources of confidence can be summarised as being increased self-awareness, which is seen to contribute to growth in confidence; self-awareness appears to derive from the extent and nature of challenge and the opportunity to reflect upon the experience.

The impact of increased confidence can often be seen in expressions of assertiveness, an increased willingness to impose oneself, which manifests in judgement and decision-making. Emerging from challenging experiences, individuals often report increased tenacity and resilience, proactivity, and motivation, inspired by a more positive attitude to themselves and their capabilities (Hannah et al., 2012). Increased confidence is particularly evident in decisions and actions relating to aspirations.

## Aspirations

Individuals consistently report a clarification of aspirations as a result of transforming experience; not only are aspirations clarified, but there can also be increased proactivity in career decision-making, research, and action. The nature and direction of stated aspirations are often revealing. Individuals do not often measure their success or employability in terms of securing a position or role; rather, they convey a sense of aspirations being *enhanced, enriched, amplified*, and *strengthened*. Evolving aspirations are often explained in terms of personal values, of having discovered what is important to an individual, and feeling empowered to make career decisions that are compatible with this. It would appear that a heightened awareness of values equals clarity of aspirations, which leads to assertive career decisions.

## Reflection

Significant challenge and reflection, appropriately supported, create awareness of and develop social and self-identity, thereby facilitating career enhancement. To support individuals to reflect deeply, what Argyris (1999) refers to as understanding *how we are being*, then it is considered important that individuals are given the tools to do this. To leave experience unconsidered and without an exploration of its significance prevents the realisation of their true value to the growth of the individual. Structured reflection, which provides the opportunity to analyse behaviour and evaluate effectiveness, promotes experience-based development (DeRue et al., 2012).

The ability and motivation to engage wholeheartedly with a process of reflection that is both challenging and supportive would appear to have benefits in terms of increased confidence, authenticity, and clarity of aspirations.

## Summary

Appropriate support and challenge, underpinned by feedback and reflection, increase self-awareness, enhance confidence, and clarify aspirations, influencing the individual's authenticity and perceptions of their employability to enhance career development.

As observed by Dr Ian Carr in the preceding text, Dr Paul-Alan Armstrong also stressed the importance of self-awareness in reflection on professional identity. His research examined the importance of the imagination and the impact of the arts in terms of creating a professional identity.

## CASE STUDY 6.2

### Dr Paul-Alan Armstrong

Dr Paul-Alan Armstrong is a senior lecturer, HRM and leadership, Sunderland Business School, University of Sunderland, UK.

Dr Armstrong said that in his situation, research into how professional identity is created was formed during doctoral studies. As reflexivity has emerged as the new gold standard for qualitative researchers who reject positivist methodologies and traditional criteria of rigour, reliability, and validity (Gabriel, 2018, p. 137), he developed the concept of a reflexive digital bricolage. Dr Armstrong argues that this process is more than creative writing, as it combines images and impressions from all media that he termed *songs of praxis*, where he visualised identity using lyrical metaphors as embodiment of 'being and becoming'. He has taught the process of identity formation for undergraduate teaching at level 6 in a reflective practice module whereby students are invited to explore how their own professional identity has formed through image, songs, art, and social media. Students then present how they visualise their professional identity (Armstrong, 2018). He has developed a reflexive practitioner toolkit as part of a VC Teaching Fellowship in 2018–2019. This was presented with the 'Innovation in Teaching of Research Methodology Excellence Award' at the 15th European Conference on Research Methods in Business for a Case History 'Human Resource Reflective Project: Developing Researching Professionals'. Previously, in 2017, his research with a colleague was awarded the 'Global HRD Research Excellence Award' from the International Federation of Training and Development Organisations (IFTDO) for their case history 'Human Resource Reflective Project: Developing Researching Professionals' (Armstrong and Bryans, 2016). This practice has been part of the pedagogy for a core module on the MSc HRM programme, where the practice has extended into the design of reflexive audio blogs and vlogs using artful imagination as portals and maps of reflective learning based on the development of the CIPD professional behaviours. This practice embraces metaphorical representation of poetics and personal artefacts as they capture emotions, feelings, as spirals and cycles of reflexive transformation through liminal space.

Jane Bell did not begin her career in HRM at university and explains her career journey in what follows.

## CASE STUDY 6.3

### Jane Bell

#### Jane Bell MCIPD: human resources business partner at the University of Sunderland

I was so lucky that I fell into HR; it was all a lovely accident after searching for my next steps after college. I didn't believe that university straight from college was the right step for me at that time, and so I saw a great role advertised for a big financial services organisation working within their central human resources team setting up organisational development projects. I barely knew the role that HR played at that time, and I was fortunate in that this is where I saw great leadership and was immersed in a culture of learning from day 1. I then started to develop professionally and moved on to leading projects and, through the next ten years, cut my teeth in organisational development in other subsidiaries of the organisation. In HR terms, I remained a specialist for a number of years within recruitment, talent, learning and development, and organisational development, finally then moving into more generalist roles working across a number of sectors, including FMCG, telecommunications and media, self-employed consultancy, and then finally, into my current role within a higher education institute. I also led teams from a fairly early age, which was the most enormous learning curve and experience which has enabled me to better support leaders and managers within an HR remit. I have taken time to understand the meaning of 'organisational culture' and its impact through each of my roles and organisations, how politics plays a part, and how to navigate the politics that exists at all levels.

I chose to train as a qualified coach at the end of 2009 and believe the skill of coaching and questioning is an essential part of any HR professional's toolkit. My master's research in 2014 focused on the impact of leadership in organisational effectiveness and is still my core area of passion.

My own personal journey has helped me reflect on the brand of human resources; it's such a crucial part of a business but rarely something that is sung about to our kids pre-undergraduate level as a career route. I think as HR professionals, we can do more.

I think I have brought something different to my generalist roles because of my career journey moving from specialist to generalist, a route which is lesser tread. Students at universities also develop their professional identity when working on live business projects during the research module or when working as a member of a team.

## THE MARKETING HUB AT THE UNIVERSITY OF SUNDERLAND

Sunderland Marketing Hub has recently been developed at the University of Sunderland. It is an academic facility that brings together students, businesses, and marketing academics at the university to work on real-life marketing projects. The aim of the Marketing Hub is to create connections between businesses and students to help students bridge the gap between academic study and theory to practice on real projects. During this process, students develop the skills required and start to create their professional identity.

Formal teaching is also provided in the Marketing Hub, such as starting an E-commerce business and developing a deeper awareness of content marketing. Students are currently working on a range of live projects, such as small companies moving into digital marketing, creating a brand logo, to designing the launch of a new business.

Students working on the projects have said they felt their confidence increased as they were able to put marketing theory to practice.

## CASE STUDY 6.4

### *Carol Stoker*

Carol Stoker is the Marketing Hub manager of the University of Sunderland's new marketing facility for students. Her working life started as a nurse, until 1989–2002, when she became a partner in a family-run catering butcher. She was instrumental in growing the business to become the third largest in the North-East of England. Before the World Wide Web, she worked in the marketing of the business, which included visiting potential customers, producing and distributing leaflets, advertising in specialist magazines, and telephoning restaurants/pubs/cafés. Along with this business, she went on to deliver the successful marketing of a hotel and wedding car business. After 2002, Carol embarked on a new business, for example, a non-Internet dating agency and marketing on Twitter, under the umbrella brand 'A Friendly Face'.

As with Ian, Paul-Alan, and Jane, Carol's professional identity was formed over the course of her experience in marketing. Carol said that:

> The experience I gained through running and marketing businesses, pre- and post-Internet, has enabled me to understand and deliver the needs and wants a business requires from a marketing campaign. My aim is to encourage and guide the students, ensuring they correctly interact with businesses and each other, with the aim of producing and presenting the exact requirements of that business.

Carol said that she also hopes that, during their interaction with the Marketing Hub, students will identify their professional identity. Professional identity is the constant construction of a student's journey, and monitoring their CPD, highlighting what they are doing well (and not so well), can enable them to do this. To identify their professional identity, students should see themselves as professionals within the marketing sector and have the confidence to present themselves as such. Carol believes that confidence comes with knowledge, and that this can be achieved by research and developing the knowledge, skills, attributes, and values that are similar to other members of the marketing profession. By doing so, the students will be able to identify themselves as being part of the profession.

## Task 6.1

### The vegetarian store and café: control of communications

For this task, think about the role you would undertake in terms of the control of communications during the planning for the new store. Think about who does what, when, and how.

Suggested responses are in Chapter 10.

## SUMMARY OF CHAPTER 6

In this chapter, we explored how the nature of professional identity is developed in different professions and in marketing.

In marketing, as in other professions, professional identity is self-realisation and how you present yourself within your own profession. It is built up over time and includes how you view yourself and how you interact with others within a professional situation. It is a complex mix of influences from your life experience and interactions with others. In most professions, it can be seen as the 'image of the professional' in that area, and in marketing, it can be defined as your personal brand. We discuss personal profiles and statements in the next chapter, and here we introduce how you can develop your 'brand identity'. It is important as a business professional to be authentic, and as presented by management theorists in Chapter 3, business professionals must ensure they can work effectively across different parts of the business sectors. In terms of the management theorists we have presented in previous chapters, they are their own 'brand ambassadors' of their work.

The next chapter explores the development of self-management in a marketing career.

## REFERENCES

Argyris, C. (1999) *On Organizational Learning*. 2nd Edition. Oxford: Blackwell.

Armstrong, P-A. (2018a) Reflexive digital bricolage: The art of digital reflection. In *6th International Conference on Professional Doctorates, 'Professional Doctorates in a Changing Landscape'*. London: Friends House. Unpublished. Available from: http://sure.sunderland.ac.uk/id/eprint/9338.

Armstrong, P-A. (2018b) Scholar practitioner, reflexive professionals, the ART of autobiographical professional development. *International Journal of Online Graduate Education*, 1(1), 1–14.

Armstrong, P-A. and Bryans, T. (2016) Human resource reflective project: Developing researching professionals'. In *ECRM 2016 Innovation in the Teaching of Research Methodology Excellence Awards*. London: ACPIL. ISBN 9781910810972.

Barkas, L.A. and Armstrong, P.A. (2021) *The Price of Knowledge and the Wisdom of Innocence Industry and Higher Education*. https://doi.org/10.1177/0950422211016293.

Barkas, L.A., Scott, J., Hadley, K. and Dixon-Todd, Y. (2021) Marketing students' meta-skills, and employability, between the lines of social capital in the context of the teaching excellence framework. *Education + Training*. https://doi.org/10.1108/ET-04-2020-0102.

DeRue, D.S., Ashford, S.J. and Myers, C.G. (2012) Learning agility: In search of conceptual clarity and theoretical grounding. *Industrial and Organizational Psychology: Perspectives on Science and Practice*, 5(3), 258–279. https://doi.org/10.1111/j.1754-9434.2012.01444.x.

Gabriel, Y. (2018) Interpretation, reflexivity and imagination in qualitative research. In M. Ciesielska and D. Jemielniak (Eds.), *Qualitative Methodologies in Organization Studies: Volume 1 Theories and New Approaches*. New York: Springer, pp. 137–157.

Hannah, S.T., Avolio, B.J., Walumbwa, F.O. and Chan, A. (2012) Leader self and means efficacy: A multi-component approach. *Organizational Behavior & Human Decision Processes*, 118(2), 143–161.

Kamara, S. and Moulds, A. (2020) *Developing Professional Identity in Multi-Professional Teams*. Academy of Medical Royal Colleges. Available from: Developing_professional_identity_in_multi-professional_teams_0520.pdf (aomrc.org.uk).

Scott, W.R. (2008) Lords of the dance: Professionals as institutional agents. *Organization Studies*, 29(2), 219–238. DOI: 10.1177/0170840607088151.

Stoker, C. (2023) *Insights into Developing Your Personal Identity. Students Tutorials in the Marketing Hub*. University of Sunderland. Unpublished.

Watson, D. and Barkas, L.A. (2018) Building a business clinic in higher education: Opportunities and challenges for students' skills development. *Journal of International Business Education*, 13, 237–248. ISSN 1649–4946.

## RECOMMENDED FURTHER READING

Gabriel, Y. (2018) Interpretation, reflexivity and imagination in qualitative research. In M. Ciesielska and D. Jemielniak (Eds.), *Qualitative Methodologies in Organization Studies: Volume 1 Theories and New Approaches*. New York: Springer, pp. 137–157.

Hannah, S.T., Avolio, B.J., Walumbwa, F.O. and Chan, A. (2012) Leader self and means efficacy: A multi-component approach. *Organizational Behavior & Human Decision Processes*, 118(2), 143–161.

Kamara, S. and Moulds, A. (2020) *Developing Professional Identity in Multi-Professional Teams*. Academy of Medical Royal Colleges. Available from: Developing_professional_identity_in_multi-professional_teams_0520.pdf (aomrc.org.uk).

*Authors' comments: The above three texts provide clearly explained insights into reflexivity and developing a professional identity.*

## CHAPTER 7

# Self-management in a marketing career

## SYNOPSIS AND LEARNING OUTCOMES

At the end of this chapter, successful students will be able to do the following:

1. Appreciate and promote their personal qualities.
2. Evaluate the skills required in self-management.
3. Critically appraise the job profile of a store manager and create a job advert for a manager for a new vegetarian shop and café.

## INTRODUCTION

This chapter is in two sections.

Section 1 starts with a discussion of what is meant by 'self-management' within a study and employment context. Examples of personal skills reviews are provided. You are then invited to review and assess your own skills. Section 1 concludes with an example of a competent manager's qualities.

Section 2 then invites you to create a role profile and a job advert for a manager for the new vegetarian shop and café.

## SECTION 1: SELF-MANAGEMENT

Self-management can be described as the ability to control our own thoughts and emotions and apply them positively and constructively. Being able to think carefully about our own attitudes and responsibilities and how our own behaviour could impact on others is important for successful study and employment. Being mentally stable in all work situations is often noted as a positive trait for the 'ideal manager'. As well as knowledge of the business they are in, managers need to acquire a range of skills and personal attributes. Strong conceptual and analytical skills are increasingly required in business dealings within the complex global economy, supported by the ability to visualise and activate transformation, if required (Whelan and Whitla, 2020). The global economy has opened

DOI: 10.4324/9781003365136-7

**FIGURE 7.23** Self-management.

up opportunities to vastly different cultures, and so managers, particularly in marketing, must be able to apply interpretative approaches to their strategy. Of course, managing risk in projects is an equally critical skill that business professionals endeavour to develop (Cox and Lowrie, 2021).

While 'on-the-job' training in marketing in business can give you a clear insight into how the company is managed, the knowledge and skills required in management can be initially developed during your degree studies. Learning to study at a higher level requires self-motivation, planning, and commitment – valuable qualities as you learn how to become a competent, trusted, and effective manager. Authors of study skills texts offer suggestions on how to manage your own learning. For example, Cottrell (2013) offers many practical tips on how to organise yourself and your study time and guides you through the expectations of higher-level study. Study skills planners are useful, and you can create your own timetable. Remember the advice that is often given, which is to set your own goals, then plan how you are going to achieve them. Remember, too, there are many setbacks in any business; how good are you at 'bouncing back' from disappointment or rejection and moving forward? Once you have completed your development plan, you can check your own current skills and qualities.

## Current skills and qualities

Recruitment agencies across various industrial sectors say that as well as knowledge of the role being offered, employers value transferable and soft skills, such as self-management and self-reliance; the capacity to focus and learn; the ability to communicate well with cultural understanding; time management; and the ability to work as an individual and as part of a team. Soft skills are therefore 'personality-driven', whereas in contrast, 'hard skills' are 'learning-driven' and would therefore include skills which can be taught at school or university or through training and employment – for example, the hard skills acquired in accounting and finance, data analysis, marketing, or project management.

How would you describe yourself? Would you say you are confident, friendly, and optimistic, or shy, cautious, and reserved? Or something in between?

Spend a few minutes thinking about the current skills and qualities you already have. Think about your friends – what qualities do you admire about them? Do you demonstrate similar personality traits? Perhaps consider what study skills you have that are also transferable and which soft skills you have that would be essential for future employment. If you feel you need to develop some skills, how would you do that? What plans do you have to improve on your own skills and qualities?

Perhaps consider creating a list and note some examples. Here are some suggestions to help you get started:

*People skills*. Consider your circle of friends and work colleagues: What is it you like about them? Do you have those qualities too? For example, you could write something along the following lines:
I have a good relationship with people from different cultures. I work in a local branch of a multinational company and have just been given the role of promoting some new products with colleagues in two other countries. I also learned how to work with people when I played regional- and national-level amateur football. I met people from different backgrounds, and we played together as a team, enjoying socialising outside football.
*Personality*. Think about what you can write about the kind of person you are. For example, rather than saying you can demonstrate commitment and are a 'caring person', think of an activity where you can demonstrate that quality:
For three years before my current job, I worked three days per week as a volunteer at a local old people's home, visiting older people who had no additional living relatives. This gave me insight into their very different lives to mine and taught me how to be sensitive and caring when responding to other people. Since starting work full-time, I still volunteer for several hours on a weekend and more during holidays. This is because I made many friendships with the occupants of the home and the staff.
*Skills*. Consider the various skills you have, such as numeracy and computer literacy, analysing information/data, and organising responsibilities and work you have to do.
*Time management*. Managers must organise their own time and responsibilities and make realistically timed plans – how good are you at managing your own time well?

To help you identify your own strengths, why not try to complete the following tasks at the end of the chapter?

Please see the following case studies on the importance of self-awareness

## CASE STUDY 7.1

### Gareth Trainer

Gareth Trainer is the head of the Centre for Graduate Prospects (CfGP) at the University of Sunderland. Gareth has spent over 20 years developing employability, enterprise, and entrepreneurship at Newcastle University before joining the University of Sunderland in March 2022. He was a director of Enterprise Educators UK (EEUK) for 9 years, serving for 2 years as its chair, and was co-author of the guidance on Enterprise and Entrepreneurship Education, originally published by the UK's Higher Education Quality Assurance Agency (QAA) in 2012. Gareth is a full member of the Association of Graduate Careers Advisory Services (AGCAS), a fellow of the Royal Society for the Encouragement of Arts, Manufactures, and Commerce (RSA), an assessor for the Small Business Charter, and holds an MBA alongside a degree in physiology and qualifications in management coaching and mentoring.

Gareth said that:

Graduate employability and enterprise are amongst its highest priorities in the University of Sunderland's Student Success Plan, and following a major and multiphase investment from the university's executive, the Centre for Graduate Prospects (CfGP) is intending to work with students, academics, and external organisations to support the delivery of this plan. Created in March 2022, the CfGP initially drew together the university's Careers and Employability Service (known as Sunderland Futures), its Enterprise Place and Digital Incubator support for freelancers and the self-employed, as well as its Graduate Internship scheme and support for non-statutory work placements. The CfGP has since been restructured into five functional areas: information, communication and engagement, student opportunities, entrepreneurial development, career development and academic support, and partnerships and work-integrated learning. Supported by Academic Champions for Employability and Enterprise (ACEEs) and Student Career and Skills Coaches, the core CfGP team has grown, via the introduction of additional roles, to become 36 members of staff strong within one academic year, with further investment following in subsequent years to help it realise its purpose and vision and deliver its mission. We believe that every student has the potential to achieve life-changing success and make a society-shaping impact, and to facilitate this, the CfGP is supporting embedding of employability and enterprise across the University of Sunderland, creating confident and motivated students who develop into professional, adaptable, and engaged graduates with rich and rewarding life and career prospects.

From the student perspective, evidence-based reflection is of paramount importance to this so individuals can recognise the effectiveness and impact of applying their knowledge and skills in the workplace. This supports the development of self-efficacy via an understanding of the value they can add and articulate, all of which contribute to the development and achievement of their career aspirations. Being able to know and show how the knowledge and skills gained during their challenging higher education relate to the job role at the company they are applying to is one of several crucial aspects of using employability to transition into work. We know from research and with feedback from employers of students and graduates that candidates that are unable to do this are usually unsuccessful with their applications. As a result, CfGP staff work with academics and students to ensure that this is practiced and understood.

Our research found that in addition to technical skills that are desirable but not always essential to the organisation (as many will want to train new hires in their specific or proprietary systems), employers seek to hire employees who are good communicators and who can demonstrate innovation, creativity, and adaptability, alongside the ability to work independently and in a resourceful and resilient way. A graduate's leadership skills can be demonstrated through their ability to take the initiative, but it is equally important to be able to emphatically listen, understand, and bring others with you in an authentic way. It's therefore important to consider the way you contribute to team discussions and demonstrate an ability to learn from co-team members. With the ongoing advancement of digital technologies, especially in fields like specialist marketing, for example, the ability to show understanding and application of digital skills is highly valued. It is also true that enhancing your skills by developing a commercial awareness of the industrial sector you are hoping to work in will be seen as a benefit by recruiting managers.

## CASE STUDY 7.2

### Garry Bishop

Garry comes from the North-East of England and now lives in Cambridgeshire. He has had a professional career in industry and higher education. He is a highly experienced and qualified coach working online supporting recent graduates, postgraduates, and early-year professionals in their career search and transition to work. He has clients UK-wide and in Europe.

He coaches clients to help them move from feeling discontented to confidently moving forward to achieve their career aspirations. He has helped numerous graduates develop or change their careers. Brittany from Swansea said, 'I have found

Garry easy to engage with, flexible in his approach, willing to listen, and above all, he enabled me to define a way forward for myself.' Michael from Northumbria said, 'I felt uplifted that we covered a lot of ground and made important progress in a relatively short space of time.' Garry supports the Sunderland Futures' (2023) research. He believes in the power of evidence-based reflection in order to help graduates recognise the effectiveness of the application of their knowledge and skills in the workplace. Regular self-reflection, using sound evidence to properly recognise achievements at work, supports robust well-being and growth in the self-confidence needed for a happy and successful career.

Once his clients have started to see how self-reflection can show how their knowledge and skills make them very employable, some of them said they felt like 'imposters'. The term 'imposter syndrome' was first created in 1978 when Drs Clance and Imes were working with high-achieving women who were experiencing anxiety and stress. Clance and Imes's (1978) research explored why this was the case and found that the women had suffered from lack of self-confidence and self-esteem from early childhood and consequently never felt 'good enough'. Each individual had complex self-esteem issues which were buried in their coping mechanisms and intensive work attitude but surfaced as stress; the therapies were equally individualised but generic, while they found that they felt better being able to talk about their feelings. Once they realised they were not alone in feeling like an imposter, the women were able to accept the fact that their success was deserved. Clance and Imes's early studies in the 1970s found the 'imposter syndrome' more prevalent amongst women, but in his work, Garry said that the best thing you can do when planning on applying for a job is to reflect on what you have done and justly recognise your own achievements, work on building your own self-confidence and self-belief, and keep mentally 'tip-top' (Bishop, 2023).

People are hired for their knowledge, skills, and abilities (KSAs) that the company requires. Hiring is a costly and lengthy process in order to ensure the right person is hired for the role being advertised. The occupation of 'firefighter' is now open to both male and females, while in the past it was a male-only occupation, simply because of the heavy weight of equipment involved, such as hoses used for water or the breathing apparatus necessary at times comprising of one or two oxygen cylinders.

The following case study is a detailed example of how you can reflect on your knowledge and skills in your career development. Once you have considered your knowledge and skills in detail, you can then decide on which key aspects could form a summary for a personal profile for a CV.

## CASE STUDY 7.3
### *Mohammad Adwan*

As a PhD student at the University of Sunderland, completing his study this year (2023) into crises/risk management in the aviation industry, Mohammad Adwan shares in what follows extracts from his personal portfolio where he highlights his decision-making along his career journey. He reflects on how he learned to develop his knowledge and skills as a manager and leader in the hospitality sector.

### Career summary

Over the last 12 years, I have been working in the hospitality sector, where I have worked in both air (aviation) and ground (hotels) hospitality. My last position at ground hospitality was as a front desk manager. This is where I have developed most of my skills and competencies after 7 years of working with multinational hotel chains. I then decided to take the opportunity and try new experiences, where I became a first-class cabin crew member in

**FIGURE 7.24** Photo of Mohammad Adwan.

one of the leading airlines in the Middle East. It was a different experience requiring a new set of skills and competencies. I believe I am one of those who strive for knowledge and learning new things. Getting out of my comfort zone was not a big challenge for me. Whenever I feel there is nothing new to learn in any place, I start looking for ways to acquire new knowledge; however, there might be advantages and disadvantages for such behaviour. On the one hand, it is always a great motivation to get into a new experience and learn new things – for me, it was always a motivation for higher performance – but on the other hand, the lack of consistency in one organisation or position may cause a slow progression in one's career path. I would always choose learning new things and getting to know new people over a high position with less knowledge and experience.

### The importance of reflection

Reflection is the means of exploring an experience using thoughts, feelings, or behaviours to understand its meaning while or after it occurs. Self-regulation depends on reflection to help you learn how to cope in environments where efficient behaviours are flexible to change and adaptation. On the other hand, critical thinking is questioning why certain behaviours and actions accrued (Cunliffe, 2004). A reflective manager is the one who can watch, step back, and realise what is going on, find new insights, and communicate the experience gained with others, besides admitting into the review non-traditional sources of intelligence or information, including emotions (Klimoski, 2007).

Mohammad Adwan goes on to say: Against this background, I may identify myself, in terms of competences and skills, as a forward-thinking hospitality professional who takes pride in influencing people's careers and lives – possessing drive, ambition, and broad knowledge of organizing, managing, and supporting day-to-day activities required for running operations; flexible with sophisticated teamworking ethics; over 12 years successfully operating and regulating functions that involve enhancing guests', colleagues', and owners' experiences. I have been known for my excellent soft skills and productive partnership with management, contributing to implementing organisations' objectives with multinational corporations.

During my working in the hospitality sector, I have filled positions which required me to handle sensitive financial reports which used to be sent daily to senior management and owners; even though it was not an area of interest, a module such as financial management and control did help widen my knowledge about many financial aspects, such as ration analysis and budgeting. On the other hand, value creation in organisations, that is, managing operations and marketing, was one of the most successful modules to me; it allowed me to apply my professional expertise as an 'operations manager' and provide recommendations. I have used a case study from a factory to reflect on learning outcomes, such as capacity management, product designs, transformational process, and operation analysis; on the other hand, the module allows you to reflect on the marketing perspective, such as marketing environments, PESTEL analysis, and TOWS matrix, besides providing recommendations. In this module, I have achieved the highest results from the expected learning outcomes. The unique thing about the innovation, entrepreneurship, and technology transfer module is that I have learned more about the mechanism and structure of writing an article, which I was able to do by the end of the module as I tried to apply the learning outcomes to write about hotels' innovation, based on my experience in one of the hotels which I worked for previously. Students are increasingly facing a complex reality in organisations in which problem-solving skills are required; hence, they must develop skills in more advanced processes in order to promote critical thinking and problem-solving (Cope, 2003).

## Student placement in the Marketing Hub at the University of Sunderland

While studying at the university, Mohammad applied and was successful for a year's work placement in the Marketing Hub at the University of Sunderland. He notes in the following his feelings at the end of the year:

By the end of the placement, I was able to provide an operations manual, a standard operating procedures guide, forms and formats, and online samples designed specifically for the Marketing Hub, which was highly appreciated by senior management, alongside my overall performance during the placement. An example of feedback from a senior management I am proud of follows:

Wow, excellent work, Mohammad. You have obviously undertaken significant work to identify how the university operates and how the Sunderland Marketing Hub can work therein. There are some great recommendations in there in terms of the roles needed, standard operating procedures, and moving the Hub forward.

### Self-assessment tool

Mr Adwan continues: A personality profile tool was helpful for me to identify the key areas in which I can develop and take actions; it provided me with useful information about my working style and gave me a better understanding of my approach with activities, relationships, and decisions. However, the level of agreement about the statements varies from one to another. Based on the results, it appears that I like to prepare well and prefer to know why and how things happen; gain great pleasure from improving upon existing techniques, with the objective of maximizing efficiency and cost-effectiveness; while my commitment to obligations comes much less in words and much more in getting things organised and done. Despite my matter-of-factness, I will sometimes experience a private reaction to something I sense is wrong, and if I articulate this, it can come as a surprise to those around me.

I am dependable and responsible, with a high sense of duty. I am usually neat, tidy, and orderly, both at work and at home. Whatever I am doing, I will accomplish with orderliness and reliability. I am a good organiser and seek to control the world around me with structure and discipline. I am responsible and faithful to my commitments and obligations. I am thorough, systematic, and hard-working and very careful that rules and precedents are honoured. I systematically set about achieving my scheduled goals on time in an efficient and effective manner.

My strong sense of personal values may make me reserved around strangers whose values I feel may conflict with my own. I like concrete facts, have a good memory for detail, and usually learn best from 'hands-on' experiences. I rely on what I can hear, see, and know from first-hand experience. In order to perform at my best, I prefer specific and detailed instructions before starting a task. My work has to contribute to things that matter to me, and I tend towards perfectionism only when I care deeply enough. Outwardly quiet, reserved, and detached, inwardly I am constantly absorbed in analysing problems or situations. I take my commitments and obligations seriously. I value and adhere to established routines and procedures, and for me there will always be some work yet to be completed. My strength is my ability to gather technical information, which gives me the potential to become an excellent researcher. Despite my quiet demeanour, I tend to thrive on excitement. I am concerned with schedules and systems and appear to some to be a very private person. Because I live by principles and rules, I am very consistent and dependable. I prefer practical work that can be tackled step-by-step. I am likely to exhibit impatience with someone who is disorganised or inconsistent. My common sense nurtures within me a practical ability when it comes to dealing with people and things.

## Interacting with others

The preference indicator in the personality assessment tool shows that I am amenable, patient, and friendly; I tend to build close, low-key relationships with a small number of associates in the work environment. I may need to be more outspoken and more direct with most people, not just those with whom I am close. I prefer to play a supporting role at work in a loyal and conscientious way. By demanding conformity to my customary way of doing things, I could discourage more creative or innovative approaches. Ever concerned with efficiency ('a place for everything and everything in its place'), I may neglect the human element, unwittingly causing stress in the process. I need to be aware of being taken advantage of by other people. I will often do without something rather than reach out to others to get it. I may seek to reduce my personal needs rather than be dependent on other people. I am seen as a gentle, caring, and sensitive person who keeps many of my intensely personal ideals and values to myself. I follow necessary systems and procedures and can be very impatient with others who are less inclined to do so. I prefer to build close relationships with small groups of people and like to retain the familiar and predictable. By remaining open-minded to untested or unconventional solutions, I would develop greater tolerance for differences and end up being more effective. I avoid interactions that will make me highly visible to others or where I have to perform or compete for attention. I am quiet, reserved, steady, dependable, and caring, and in my relationships – as with everything else – my strong sense of duty predominates. I am not always keen to express how I feel. Preferring to care for others and to help them in practical and tangible ways, I use my quietly personal warmth to communicate this feeling.

## Decision-making

I am a good mediator or peacekeeper because I can agree while not being fully drawn to any one view. I have a tendency to separate out the different components of my life, wanting predictability and preferring to know various options in advance. My quiet demeanour often allows me to get agreement to my alternative solutions. I take a personal approach to living, assessing events through the personal values and ideals which govern my life. I am prepared to make decisions through group consensus. With my moderate, affable stance, I am considerate, patient, and willing to go along with those I consider friends. I am usually aware of the need to comply with the established view. My decisions tend to be made only after I have gathered sufficient supporting data. My natural introversion does not prevent me from making critical and incisive comments with conviction and presence. My practical nature and acceptance of established procedures ensures I am dependable and consistent. I am not usually prepared to commit to high-risk decisions. I am observant of the small jobs that need to be done and will often offer to do them or just do them automatically. When I perceive that something needs to be done, I will accept responsibility for implementing it. I make better decisions when other people I know share my values. I see myself as realistic, practical, and matter-of-fact, although others may not always see the practicality of some of my decisions.

## Key strengths and weaknesses

This section in the analytical tool helps you see what strengths you can bring to an organisation and what areas to work on.

Examples of my strengths are finishing things that I have started; being supportive, being steadfast, and encouraging others; and being trustworthy.

Examples of my weaknesses are: I find it difficult to refuse requests from people as I wish to avoid threatening good interpersonal relationships; I may worry unduly and can be prone to pessimism at times.

## Effective communications

Some examples of the key strategies which will lead to effective communication with me are ensuring a logical reason for any changes and giving me verifiable facts. Recognising the characteristics of the opposite type of personality can help in developing strategies for personal growth and enhanced interpersonal effectiveness.

The preference indicator helps you recognise traits of opposite personality types, and in the workplace, and as a manager, this is very helpful, of course. Understanding how others think/respond is a very good skill to develop when working with diverse team members.

## Career advice to new students

Mr. Adwan continues: During the MBA, I participated in a webcast to speak about the MBA experience at the University of Sunderland (UOS); it was the first time I had spoken to the camera. During the interview, I talked about the course overview regarding the main attraction to study a business-related subject; the key differences between studying at the UOS and other universities; the university's facilities; and its location. The interview discussed employability aspects, such as the professional areas of employment one might consider after completing the course. I also had the chance to speak about the placement programme and my role as operations manager in the Sunderland Marketing Hub and other opportunities at the university, such as the guest speaker programme. Finally, I got the chance to impart a piece of wisdom to those students who are worried about balancing a degree workload with family or work commitment, where I said: 'Believe in yourself. Determine your priorities. Patience is key. Knowledge is power.' It was a great opportunity for me to enhance my own self-confidence and speak my thoughts about the MBA experience at the University of Sunderland.

Now, after reading Mohammad's detailed self-appraisal, why not look back at the qualities of a good manager (Chapter 3) and see where you would be able to match these against your own list of skills and qualities? Which aspects do you think are critical for a manager of the new vegetarian shop and café?

In the following section you are invited to identify the desired knowledge and skills required for this post in order to decide on how best to advertise for a new employee.

## SECTION 2

### Example

Imagine the new shop and café will soon be open and you need to recruit a shop and café manager. You would need to create a job profile and an advert for the new store. Before you start, you would review the company's standard practices. In our imaginary company, as the vegetarian shops and cafés will have recruited many people, their central human resource department will offer guidance and suggest templates.

Some companies have been very creative or even quirky in promoting themselves – not easy to do well, of course! Have a check of job adverts in your local area: Are there any that stand out as particularly welcoming? What is it about the role that catches your attention? If you are serious about a marketing career, you will have strong creative skills and can put them to good use in the design of a wonderful advert! Remember: all companies want to attract talented, capable people to boost the success and development of the organisation.

So where would you start? How would you market the company in the advert? Perhaps you could start by saying how successful it is and promote the benefits of working for the vegetarian shop and café chain as it has been listed as one of the best places to work. (Think about applying the marketing 'hooks' from Chapters 1 and 2.) Consider the impact of promoting the employment package, the above-average salary, training, and development opportunities (once experienced, you could apply for a senior regional manager position), health benefits, generous holiday allowance, and company pension scheme.

A person applying for the role would need to review the key accountabilities and responsibilities of the role. How would you decide what these are? What are your priorities of what you want in our store manager? Look back to your notes on what you think makes a competent manager, and review the previous section on what we think are some of the valued qualities in such an individual.

Perhaps consider completing the following tasks?

### Task 7.1

What are your best qualities? Write down as many as possible. For example: flexible, articulate, loyal, consistent, thoughtful, accurate, and so on.

Once you have your list, put the skills and qualities under headings such as 'people skills', 'technical knowledge', and 'research skills'.

## Task 7.2

Then, when you have your own list, put them in order of priority. To do this, think about how you could develop your own personal profile. A personal profile is a simple summary of who and where you are now.

Drawing on your own qualities as a base, what else would you want in the manager for the new shop and café?

## Task 7.3

Here is a basic job advert. How can you develop it to attract the right candidate for the new shop?

## FICTITIOUS JOB ADVERTISEMENT

### Vegetarian shop and café manager

The vegetarian shop and café chain is expanding, and we have an exciting opportunity for a manager for a new shop opening very soon. We are looking for an enthusiastic candidate, ideally with some store and/or café management experience. This is not essential, however, as training will be given. You will have skills in food and drink preparation and food safety, with supporting qualifications. You will have excellent communication skills and, in addition, experience of working with vendors and suppliers. Working in a rota system is a requirement of the role, as once in the post, you would need to recruit an assistant shop manager and other staff to work alongside with you. The vegetarian shop and café chain offers excellent benefits, training and a career development scheme, a competitive salary of XXXXX (this would be appropriate to the region for similar roles at that time), generous holiday entitlement, and a pension scheme. If you feel this is the role for you, please apply to the online email address (stated here) by xx month/year.

After considering the qualities of the 'ideal manager', how could you develop the advert to attract the candidate you are looking for? What else do you think could be important to attract the best person for the role? To answer these questions, you may choose to consider a checklist of essential and desirable criteria, then you could give a weighting to each criterion of what you think are essential versus desirable knowledge and skills. This list will assist you in creating questions when you interview potential candidates.

Suggested responses are in Chapter 10.

## SUMMARY OF CHAPTER 7

In this chapter we have discussed some aspects of self-management and how you may choose to plan the development of your own knowledge and skills. We have also provided an in-depth case study detailing the development of an individual's career, that of Mohammad Adwan, where he has used self-assessment and evidence-based self-reflection in order to achieve his career aspirations. The task in this chapter invited you to create a role profile and a job advert for a manager for the new 'vegetarian shop and café'.

The next chapter explores managing others in marketing.

# REFERENCES

Bishop, G. (2023) *Online Graduate Career Coach*. About Garry – Garry Bishop. Available from: Online Graduate Career Coach - Garry Bishop

Clance, P.R. and Imes, S. (1978) The imposter phenomenon in high achieving women: Dynamics and therapeutic intervention. *Psychotherapy Theory, Research and Practice*, 15(3), 241–247. https://psycnet.apa.org/doi/10.1037/h0086006.

Cope, J. (2003) Entrepreneurial learning and critical reflection. *Management Learning*, 34, 429–450.

Cottrell, S. (2013) *The Study Skills Handbook*. 4th Edition. Hampshire: Palgrave Macmillan.

Cox, T. and Lowrie, K. (2021) From the editors: Setting risk management priorities. *Risk Analysis*, 40(8), 1255–1495. https://doi-org.ezproxy.sunderland.ac.uk/10.1111/risa.13811.

Cunliffe, A.L. (2004) On becoming a critically reflective practitioner. *Journal of Management Education*, 28, 407–426.

Klimoski, R.J. (2007) Introduction: Promoting the 'practice' of learning from practice. *Academy of Management Learning and Education*, 6, 493–494.

University of Sunderland. (2020) *Register for Our Webcast – University of Sunderland*. Available from: www.sunderland.ac.uk/open-days/webcasts/register-for-our-webcast/?gid=623577313244658789410a86d7bb8e0a473961 (Accessed 24 June 2020).

University of Sunderland Futures. (2023) Available from: Sunderland Futures | The University of Sunderland.

Whelan, J. and Whitla, S. (2020) *Visualising Business Transformation: Pictures, Diagrams, and the Pursuit of Shared Meaning*. Abingdon: Routledge.

# RECOMMENDED FURTHER READING

Connett, W. and Kindness, D. (2023) *Hard Skills: Definition, Examples, and Comparison to Soft Skills*. Available from: Hard Skills: Definition, Examples, and Comparison to Soft Skills (investopedia.com).
*Authors comment: An easy to access website with clear guidance on hard and soft skills*
Cottrell, S. (2013) *The Study Skills Handbook*. 4th Edition. Hampshire: Palgrave Macmillan.
*Authors comment: A very good book providing guidance on effective study.*
Pratt, M.K. (2023) *Soft Skills (Definition)*. Available from: What is soft skills? | Definition from TechTarget.
*Authors comment: Another easy to access website with clear guidance on developing soft skills.*

## CHAPTER 8

# Managing others in marketing

## SYNOPSIS AND LEARNING OUTCOMES

At the end of this chapter, successful students will be able to do the following:

1. Apply the cognitive skills of critical thinking and analysis when evaluating different approaches to leading and managing marketing teams.
2. Demonstrate knowledge and ability to evaluate leadership styles and strategies to apply in an organisation and evaluate tools and techniques associated with leading and managing a team promoting a marketing campaign.

## INTRODUCTION

In the previous chapters, we have explored different theories of management and leadership and looked at ways you may analyse and develop your own skills. In this chapter we discuss how the various aspects of effective management and leadership can be applied to managing people in marketing teams within organisations.

## MANAGING PEOPLE IN ORGANISATIONS

The structure of an organisation reflects how employees are managed. Employment law has developed to ensure organisations comply with legislation on peoples' working rights, such as well-being, health and safety, data protection, and general working conditions (Gov.UK., 2023). So it is important in the UK that managers and human resources personnel are compliant with this legislation. For overseas employment, it is necessary for managers to adhere to the employment legislation of their particular locality.

Studies of organisational behaviour and development began in scientific management research, and later humanistic models evolved, as discussed in Chapter 3; so over the past few decades, human resource management has grown into a specialist area. You

DOI: 10.4324/9781003365136-8

**FIGURE 8.25** Managing others.

may recall from your reading of the influential management theorists how the interest in human interactions at work evolved from scientific theories of management, whereby modern theories were influenced by the need to improve productivity through motivating employees. Human resource management (HRM) departments, therefore, developed and are concerned with managing an organisation's employees, and as working practices have become so diverse, so too has the nature of the functions of HRM. Managers of different departments and teams would work closely with the HRM department. As modern business has diversified and expanded, so too has the core functions of HRM, which can be said is to attract, recruit, and retain staff but now includes research by professional bodies that explore ways to 'champion for better working lives' (CIPD, 2023).

Employee relations may be defined within the context of the values inherent in organisational development. Managing employee relations is therefore critical as part of 'better working lives' for all. Many organisations work by encompassing different cultures, so an appreciation of how cultural values vary is helpful to ensuring good employee relations. Hofstede's (1991) research explored cultural differences in society and found that different societies placed importance on various aspects of individualism versus collectivism and femininity or masculinity.

The recent global Covid pandemic (World Health Organisation, 2023) impacted greatly on how organisations were able to continue to operate, resulting in many employees working remotely, and this affected how teams can work together. However, remote working is not new, and even before the pandemic, many employees in different sectors have been working remotely. The key to successful management of remote workers is for managers to ensure clear communications and not to assume every team member knows the priorities of their team, to be more of a mentor than a manager, and most importantly, to focus on outcomes rather than activity (Gleeson, 2023).

Working successfully in teams is a critical part of many organisations, and much more can be achieved if the group of people work together to formulate positive, team dynamics; however, this is easier said than done! In an organisation, a group of people can be connected in various ways, but a team should collaborate in order to reach a common goal. Working in groups can be effective if each member achieves their individual goals, but individual and collaborative accountability is only possible if the team shares their purpose and goals.

Motivation is a fundamental part of ensuring teams work well, but understanding the factors that nurture motivation is exceedingly complex. Research into motivation may focus on the *process* of motivation or *aspects* of the content of it. Abraham Maslow is acknowledged as a leading theorist on how motivation impacts on how people work. He was born in New York and studied as a psychologist and behavioural scientist and also worked in industry (Maslow, 1970). His research, termed the 'hierarchy of needs', is acknowledged as being a leading influence in further studies into motivation. Maslow's hierarchical theory of human needs has therefore influenced management and marketing theories ever since. Basically, Maslow (1970) argued, people are motivated by basic survival needs, such as the requirement for food and sleep, safety, love, and self-esteem; eventually, the need for self-fulfilment takes precedence. Other scholars, such as Alderfer (1972) and Drucker (1974), although they agreed with Maslow, however, argued that the needs were on a continuum, not *necessarily* in a hierarchy. Early studies of motivation then looked at physical motivations, such as survival, hunger, and shelter. Further research on organisational development by Schein (1985) then led to a classification model of motivation that drew on Maslow's studies but stressed the importance and influence of the psychological contract between the employee and the organisation. That is, the respective expectations each employee has of each other, and the management has of them. Schein's work (1985) had two aspects that have entered the language on management research, which are the 'psychological contract' and the 'career anchor', both aspects exploring how employees feel motivated. The critical part here is, the psychological contract includes the company's and the employees' *expectations* of each other. Schein's (1985) use of the term 'anchor' referred to aspects of how employees view the importance of progress in their careers, such as technical competence, having confidence in management, and autonomy in the job they are doing.

Similar to Maslow's (1970) and Schein's (1985) research, McGregor (1960) studied managers' interpretation of employees' behaviour and developed his 'theory X and theory Y model'. Douglas McGregor was an American psychologist who specialised in human behaviour, and his studies explored the issues in authoritarian management, termed 'theory X', and participative management, termed 'theory Y'. In his work, McGregor argued that people are motivated by self-fulfilment (theory Y), and that a management style focused on direction and control, whether hard or soft (theory X), is detrimental to an organisation's success because employees are demotivated or fearful and thereby not fulfilling their potential. McGregor (1967) did not state that all authority was inappropriate but stressed that employees are more likely to exercise self-direction to support an organisation's objectives if they are motivated through a 'theory Y' model that encourages innovation, participation, and autonomy.

Chris Argyris worked with Donald Schon (1978) to research how an organisational goal may be contradictory. For example, employees may be encouraged to take the initiative but still be expected to follow the company's rules. Thus, Argyris and Schon (1978) developed their model I and model II theories to explain how managers addressed such contradictions. Argyris and Schon's study found that in model I, when managers defend themselves but impose changes on employees, distrust and repression build, resulting in defensive routines and restricted learning/development, in what they termed 'single-loop' learning. To avoid this, it is necessary to adopt a model II approach and move towards a better culture, through a process of what they termed 'double-loop' learning. For this to happen, it is necessary for the manager to find out how they can create trust in communication and can invite discussion and collaboration (Argyris and Schon, 1978; Argyris, 1985).

Other studies of motivation, including Herzberg's, examined the impact on motivation of the 'hygiene factors' of work, such as company policies, working conditions, salary, status, and job security. Frederick Herzberg, an American psychologist, and his colleagues Mausner and Synderman (1959) are acknowledged in the management literature for their insights into the importance of a positive working environment. Theirs was one of the early studies into the importance of employees' mental health related to job satisfaction and what they termed 'job enrichment'.

Amongst others, the aforementioned theories of motivation have influenced current working practices in organisations that allow flexibility in working hours and more choice of which company benefits an employee may choose. Ensuring teams can work effectively and positively is a key part of a successful strategy, but while a manager may claim to be proactive – while still 'being in charge' – this pretence of proactiveness is often reactiveness in disguise. True proactiveness comes from seeing how we contribute to our own problems; it is a product of our way of thinking and not our emotional state. Learning to work effectively in teams often allows us to view our own issues about the task in hand.

## TEAM BUILDING

Team building is therefore paramount in any organisation. Sometimes, even experienced managers will lay claim to the myth that their talent for 'good team building' is one of their successful management skills! Efforts may fail, as all too often employees are fighting for turf – but maintain the *appearance* of the image of a cohesive team. If there is disagreement, people with serious reservations may avoid stating them publicly; joint decisions are watered down, compromised, or one person's view is foisted on the group. Many management teams break down under pressure, as noted by Chris Argyris (1985) when he researched learning in management teams and stated, '[A] team may function well with routine issues, but confronted with complex or threatening issues – the team goes to pot.' Or when asked by Senge, '.[W]hen was the last time someone in an organisation was rewarded for raising difficult questions about the company's current policies rather than solving problems?' (Senge, 1990, p. 25). Even if we are uncertain, we learn to protect ourselves from the pain of appearing uncertain or ignorant. The very process blocks out new understandings which might threaten us; Argyris calls this 'skilled incompetence'. In other words, such teams which are full of people who are incredibly proficient at keeping themselves from learning (Argyris, 1985).

Is there a secret to successful team building? Perhaps an effective marketing team may be able to answer this question! Employees can work in groups, but not all work groups make integrated teams. A manager may have responsibility for a number of different groups that are actually independent, even though they contribute to the organisation's business. Kurt Lewin (1952) is recognised in the management literature as one of the earliest researchers into group dynamics. As a social psychologist, he explored how leadership styles impacted on groups, and this led to his 'force-field theory', where he noted how the environmental forces influenced people working in groups, whether or not factors in the work situation (in the 'field') were aiding or inhibiting change. Tuckman's (1965) model of group dynamics is frequently cited in the management literature as he identified the different stages of group working: forming, where the group starts to work together through the stages of action, which he then termed, storming, norming, and performing. In working together, Edward De Bono (1971) stressed the critical importance of lateral thinking and creativity, arguing that we only use lateral thinking 5% of the time, and vertical thinking for the other 95% of the time. Managers, in their work with teams, De Bono argued, must foster creativity, and he developed his ideas in his 1985 work *Six Thinking Hats*.

Developing creative approaches to team management and particularly to marketing teams can be enabled if the team roles and characteristics are supportive. Belbin's (2023) research identified nine types of human behaviour that characterises how people work in team roles. She called these resource investigator, team-worker, and coordinator (the social roles); plant, monitor evaluator, and specialist (the thinking roles); and shaper, implementer, and completer finisher (the action or task roles) (Belbin, 2023). She argued that it is *not* necessary for the manager or team leader to treat everyone the same, because each member of the team would gravitate to a role that was best for them. The secret, of course, is working out how to ensure the different personalities in the team can stay motivated and on task!

Please see the example case study of how managing and leadership can be combined in the hospitality sector.

## CASE STUDY 8.1

*Alessandro Ferraza*

### Managing teams in the hospitality sector

Alessandro Ferrazza is currently a lecturer in the business faculty, teaching postgraduate students at Sunderland University in London. He is undertaking his professional doctorate, researching how addressing motivation can influence positive change in management practices. Alessandro is a fellow member of the Institute of Hospitality (IoH), a chartered manager and fellow member of the Chartered Management Institute (CMI), and a fellow of the Institute of Leadership and Management (ILM). Alessandro's career started in hotels after graduation, and he has worked with global organisations in a variety of senior and executive management roles, such as food and beverage director, front of house director, and regional account director. Although Alessandro has predominantly worked in the UK and Italy, he has also extensively held posts with co-operations in France and Switzerland. Whilst in Switzerland, between 1984 and 1986, Alessandro was in charge of managing all hospitality services for Union Bank of Switzerland (UBS) centre of excellence in Zurich and the European Head Office in London. While in Italy, from 1993 to 2001, he was a member of the board of directors for Princess Pallavicini in Rome, managing two of the Princess organisations. In 2001 and up until a career change into higher education in 2019, Alessandro worked with Compass Group Plc initially as a general manager, to then move to other roles, reaching the height of his career with the company as regional account director. In this role, the author was able to extend his knowledge to strategically support the division with a multimillion-pound business.

**FIGURE 8.26** Alessandro Ferraza.

Alessandro writes in what follows about his experience of leading and managing different functional teams as well as in marketing:

> Over the last decade, my business in contract catering, a devolved business from the hospitality industry, turned over close to £67 million per year with a team of 500+ staff managed through 23 direct reports. The principal element for managing such large resources is ensuring that the senior team has a clear brief and direction of operation. My stance had been for the manager to discuss their solutions and allow them to be in charge of their destiny. My senior team was always able to make independent decisions for any operational call, which said, however, for any decision that would have a direct impact on the division's bottom line, a case would need to be presented and agreed with myself and my finance director. One of the core principles I introduced early on, when I took over the region, was to implement a strong succession plan, thus giving all employees a chance to develop their skills. This consisted of enabling junior managers to acquire the relevant knowledge and skills to progress to middle management roles, and middle managers to move to senior positions. The system was supported by a large number of educational activities; as not all skills can be acquired on the job, most of the team regularly spent time between colleges and universities to gain the

relevant theoretical knowledge to apply on the job. My annual spend on education was in the region of £45,000–50,000. Over time, our team was the most advanced and educated of the whole company. I have always been of the opinion that I rather companies try and poach our team members because of their capabilities and skills, clearly recognizing the greater level of professional delivery the team was able to deliver.

Alessandro went on to say:

This process gave all employees an equal opportunity to progress; it also helped enhance the feeling of belonging and attainment within the team. The outcome was, the whole division worked in unison as a single entity and thus met all the key performance indicators each year. In fact, over the 12 years of my employment with the organisation, my region never lost a single contract. We worked constantly to maintain excellent relationships with our clients, and this helped retain current business but also develop new contracts. For example, we took over contracts with a pure food service-delivery contract, but by midterm of the contract, we had also renegotiated to incorporate other services, such as refuse collection and recycling, cleaning, security, soft and hard facilities management (FM).

I was also responsible for client retention and sales. For this, I engaged the support of two senior sales managers and a bid writer. The process was not only to ensure that we offered our clients the best possible option but also that we professionally presented the solution. To do this, the chief executive officer implemented what he called a white hat and black hat system. The first, the white hat, addressed the needs of the current clients in the retention process, whilst the second, black hat, was aimed at a new prospective client. This system was aligned in terms of bid presentation and improved our sales ratio from one-fifth to three-fifths in Europe and from one-third to one-half in the USA.

The experience gained during my professional career helped me learn how to lead and manage staff in my teams. My management style is influenced by theorists such as Mintzberg (1973) and Drucker (1946), but also some real inspiration came from Ricardo Semler, and I would say that the best way to manage teams is through inspiring and setting examples, through letting go and transforming managers in trusted allies, and allowing people to develop and deliver to their full potential.

(Ferrazza, 2023)

This concludes the summary of Alessandro Ferrazza's career.

Please see the following example case study of how teamworking is integrated in the film industry.

## CASE STUDY 8.2

*Benjamin Spence*

### Working in film marketing

**FIGURE 8.27**  Benjamin Spence at King Arthur 2017.

### Personal Photo: Benjamin at a promotional event for King Arthur. Legend of the Sword

Benjamin Spence is currently working as an associate tutor at the University of Sunderland while he is completing his PhD studies in marketing (2023). He summarises his career as follows:

**Summary of Benjamin's career**

My undergraduate degree was in magazine journalism, and I was able to base my dissertation around a weekly club event, which I project-managed at that time in the local area. The event was targeted towards the LGBTQ+ community and allies and created a safe space, launching with an 'LGBTQ+' prom. The launch of the magazine complimented the events promotional mix, which included substantial social media engagement and PR via local news outlets. Following a placement opportunity at a national magazine in London, I continued as a blogger for the publication for several years and also became a staff writer for an international publication. These opportunities coincided with my main passion of film and marketing, working in the cinema industry for 12 years. During this time, I was able to re-locate to London and work in the heart of film marketing in Leicester Square. Each week I led and managed teams, hosting several high-profile events, such as red carpet film premiers with global A-listers in attendance. Personal highlights have included meeting Brad Pitt, Goldie Hawn, Angelina Jolie, Quentin Tarantino, Mark Hamill, Channing Tatum, Bruce Willis, Hugh Jackman, Russell Crowe, and Dame Helen Mirren, to name but a few. As part of the marketing team, I assisted with social media management and was involved in creating a buzz leading up to the event and launched the brand's 'Live from the Red Carpet', offering real-time insights directly from the red carpet via social media.

Benjamin stresses the importance of managing others and teamworking when communications involve different projects and teams. He held regular update meetings to record and update progress and offers the following marketing insights:

> Working in film marketing, I would argue, is a unique experience when compared to any other industry. Leading and managing teams is very complex. You must consider the 'product' element of the marketing mix: the feature film itself is the product, which can, of course, vary from comedy to animation to horror to action to musicals, all targeting different demographics. One marketing campaign may focus efforts on the senior demographic, whereas another may be on the 'girls' night out' crowd, with other campaigns focused on younger audiences. This is all determined by the product offering: the film itself.
>
> In the cinema environment, the film line-up also changes on a weekly basis, with new features entering the mix and older or less-popular features departing. Each film is also brought to market by various distributors, who act as the intermediary between the filmmakers and the cinemas. Therefore, film marketers work with different partners for different products when constructing marketing strategies for the film. Furthermore, with satellite technology, cinemas can also stream live concerts, theatre performances, television events, and football matches, thereby opening up to wider segments and differing marketing efforts.
>
> As a marketer in the industry, you gain access to the film distributors slate (upcoming line-up) annually, so cinemas are in position to plan marketing efforts effectively. A perk of this includes invitations to film conferences, where you can watch several films well in advance of release to the general public. This allows for the foundations of formulating local marketing campaigns and considering any potential local partners, that is, bars, restaurants, car dealers,

children's entertainers, pet shops, cosplay groups. Forming such relationships allows the opportunity to add to the consumers experience of visiting the cinema and differentiates the brand from market-share competitors.

Once external marketing communications have attracted the consumer to the venue, on-site marketing efforts come into play. These efforts are the responsibility of all employees, for example, when selling the format of the film, for example, IMAX, 3D, VIP (considering the 'pricing' element of the marketing mix). The banners, posters, branding of upcoming films around the venue (promotional elements) and, of course, the sales of ice creams, hotdogs, and bucket loads of popcorn! (Consider the 'place' element of the marketing mix for these retail items: Have you ever paid a premium price for these snacks? Does this mark-up provide a further revenue stream for the brand?)

Working in film marketing was a thoroughly enjoyable experience, and maintaining my contacts has allowed for this to cross over into my academic career, including film distributors as guest speakers within modules and relevant company visits. Marketing film encourages an abundance of creativity, the opportunity to develop industry relationships, skill development gained through promoting towards a wide range of demographics, and in my lucky case, the opportunity to strut around the red carpet on a weekly basis. All for social media purposes, of course.

This concludes the summary of Benjamin's career.

When working on the following task, think about the various aspects of the launch of a film that Ben described earlier. Perhaps consider how you may utilise some of the marketing approaches he presents?

## TASK 8.1: MANAGING A MARKETING CAMPAIGN – THE NEW VEGETARIAN SHOP AND CAFÉ

### How would you design and promote a marketing campaign?

### *Some guidance before you start*

Managing a marketing campaign is a complex activity, how big the budget should be to create the campaign, of course, being perhaps the key factor. You will recall from Chapter 3 that you had a budget to find and develop the stop, so you will have already allocated some funds to the marketing campaign. In management terms, planning a marketing campaign can be seen as a project, with many decisions to be made throughout the process. Much will depend on how the organisation manages its operations and what place marketing has within the structure of the organisation.

In our illustration for our imaginary vegetarian shop and café chain, we will state that there is a separate human resource management department, so in a real-life situation, they would be consulted to help with any aspect of staffing and human resource strategy/strategies.

## TIPS FOR PLANNING YOUR MARKETING CAMPAIGN!

After reflecting on Ben's comments, please review the previous chapters on marketing and work through the mnemonic MARKETING from Chapter 3, which will help remind you of the essential phases of any successful marketing campaign. Furthermore, here are some aspects you will also need to consider. First of all, the actual planning of the marketing framework; the marketing campaign is part of the overall marketing planning process, and in particular, large organisations, such as, in our imaginary case study, the head office of the vegetarian shop and café (VSC) chain, will have a strategy for this. The head office and senior management team will have a detailed strategic analysis of where they are in achieving their business goals. So you can pretend in this task that you already have knowledge of this. An organisation's past, present, and future business, therefore, are an integral part of all planning. The key questions to consider in your task are as suggested by Masterson et al. (2017), who identify seven aspects of any business that need to be addressed and which are related to a strategic gap analysis. Remember, you are acting as a vegetarian shop and café (VSC) manager here:

1. Where are you now? (You know that VSC is successful and has the resources to develop further.)
2. How did you get here? (By starting slowly and learning from mistakes and building up gradually too.)
3. Where will you be? (That is, if VSC stays as it is now.)
4. Where do you want to be? (Successful in new areas.)
5. How are you going to get there? (By planning and opening new shops.)
6. Are you getting there? (Yes, you are about to launch a new shop.)
7. Have you arrived? (Almost! 😊)

You will start with a planning and marketing communications framework – your budget will be ascertained, of course, and as in project management, you will have to work within it. (Reflect back on your previous tasks, and imagine what you think you will need in order to allocate a sufficient budget to pay for the campaign.) You will understand your buyer behaviour, and as this is a new shop, you will be working with the head office of the vegetarian shop and café (VSC), but you will be expected to design your own marketing campaign.

## REMEMBER THE MARKETING MIX!

The original marketing mix was defined by McCarthy in 1960 and popularised by Kotler (2020). It is widely known as the 4Ps: product, promotion (marketing communications), price, and place (distribution/channels). Marketing researchers have now added a further 3Ps: people, physical evidence, and process. You will need to consider the following aspects:

The importance of targeting and segmenting consumer markets.

How will you attract customers to the new shop? Consider 'push or pull' factors. How is the customer engaged?

Remember, the importance of ensuring strategies for the marketing campaign are integrated in order to ensure that the position and tools of the marketing mix are all connected to the launch of the new shop and café.

How will you decide the balance of promoting the vegetarian shop and its business in conjunction with the café and its business? Which is the better marketing strategy, do you think? To promote the shop as one service or split the advertising to emphasise both? The marketing mix could be constructed differently, for example, to draw customers to the café first, then encourage them to buy the food served from the shop, and vice versa. These would be questions you would need to consider in your marketing team.

The position and tools of the marketing mix coalesce into an overall marketing campaign, but the prominence of each individual element is variable, depending on the nature and purpose of the marketing campaign; for example, see the varying emphasis of the messages in advertisements. The tools of the marketing mix are as follows:

Advertising, sales promotion, direct marketing, personal selling, public relations, and the wider communications mix (people and other partners).

You will recall the 4Cs framework and can see how the different approaches to marketing exhibit high or low characteristics in relation to the different aspects of the 4Cs: communications, credibility, costs, and control.

Remember DRIP!

'DRIP' is the strategy to show the uniqueness of the product or service, and the acronym stands for the following:

*Differentiate*. This is to make a product or service stand out in the specific category.
*Reinforce*. To help consolidate and strengthen the previous messages.
*Inform*. To ensure that the places of purchase are identified and that product/service features and benefits are clear.
*Persuade*. To encourage further purchases.

Furthermore, how will you promote your new shop in advertisements?

Remember AIDA!

AIDA is a promotions model terminology: attention, interest, desire, and action = AIDA. The suggested responses to designing and promoting a marketing campaign are in Chapter 10.

## SUMMARY OF THE CHAPTER

In this chapter we have explored the importance of managing others through a discussion and evaluation of different approaches to managing marketing teams. We then applied leadership and management strategies to planning the promotion of a marketing campaign.

The next chapter examines the development of leadership and reflection in marketing.

# REFERENCES

Alderfer, C.P. (1972) *Existence, Relatedness, and Growth. Human Needs in Organisational Settings*. New York: Free Press.

Belbin, M. (2023) *High Performance Teams*. Belbin: High Performing Teams.

CIPD – Chartered Institute of Personnel and Development. (2023) *CIPD the Professional Body for Human Resources and People Development*. Available from: Join CIPD: How to Become a CIPD Member - CIPD | CIPD

COVID. (2023) *World Health Organisation*. WHO. Available from: WHO Coronavirus (COVID-19) Dashboard | WHO Coronavirus (COVID-19) Dashboard With Vaccination Data

De Bono, E. (1971) *Lateral Thinking for Management*. Maidenhead: McGraw Hill.

De Bono, E. (1985) *Six Thinking Hats*. London: Penguin.

Drucker, P.F. (1974) *Management: Tasks, Responsibilities, Practices*. London: Heinemann.

Ferrazza, A. (2023) *Professional Doctorate: Leadership and Management Professional Presentations – Hospitality* (April 19th) University of Sunderland. Unpublished.

Gleeson, B. (2023) *Taking Point Leadership Development I Building High-Performance Teams*. Available from: Taking Point Leadership Development I Building High-Performance Teams

Hertzberg, F., Mausner, B. and Snyderman, B. (1959) *The Motivation to Work*. New York: Wiley.

Hofstede, G. (1991) *Cultures and Organizations: Software of the Mind*. London: McGraw-Hill.

Lewin, K. (1952) *Field Theory in Social Science*. New York: Harper and Row.

Maslow, A.H. (1970) *Motivation and Personality*. New York: Harper and Row.

Masterson, R., Phillips, N. and Pickton, D. (2017) *Marketing, an Introduction*. 4th Edition. London: Sage.

McCarthy, E.J. (1960) *Basic Marketing: A Managerial Approach*. New York: McGraw-Hill.

McGregor, D. (1960) *The Human Side of Enterprise*. New York: McGraw-Hill.

McGregor, D. (1967) *The Professional Manager*. New York: McGraw-Hill.

Mintzberg, H. (1973) *The Nature of Managerial Work*. New York: Free Press.

Schein, E.H. (1985) *Organizational Culture and Leadership*. San Francisco: Jossey-Bass.

Semler, R. (1994) *Maverick! The Success Story Behind the World's Most Unusual Workplace*. London: Arrow.

Senge, P. (1990) *The Fifth Discipline: The Art and Practice of the Learning Organization*. New York: Doubleday/Currency.

Tuckman, B. (1965) Developmental sequence in small groups. *Psychological Bulletin*, 63(6), 384–399. DOI: 10.1037/h0022100. PMID 14314073.

# RECOMMENDED FURTHER READING

Belbin, M. (2023) *High Performance Teams*. Belbin: High Performing Teams.

*Authors comments: Belbin provides detailed insights into how teams can work together in a positive and effective manner.*

CIPD – Chartered Institute of Personnel and Development. (2023) *CIPD the Professional Body for Human Resources and People Development.* Available from: Join CIPD: How to Become a CIPD Member - CIPD | CIPD

*Authors comments: The CIPD has a wealth of information on professional practice.*

De Bono, E. (1971) *Lateral Thinking for Management.* Maidenhead: McGraw Hill.

*Authors comments: De Bono discusses the critical importance of clear thinking across all issues of business providing a valuable insight into the role of lateral thinking for managers.*

## CHAPTER 9

# Being a leader and personal reflector in marketing

## SYNOPSIS AND LEARNING OUTCOMES

At the end of this chapter, successful students will be able to do the following:

1. Apply the cognitive skills of critical thinking and analysis when evaluating different approaches to developing leadership skills.
2. Demonstrate understanding and the ability to undertake personal reflection.

## INTRODUCTION

In this chapter, we review some theoretical approaches to leadership development in relation to personal reflection in marketing (Kotter, 1990; Northouse, 2019). We then discuss the importance of the role of leaders of marketing teams to inspire others when creating a vision of the future for their organisation. This will be explored through the examination of the responsibility of leaders to create the direction the marketing team should take. It is also critical for leaders to establish realistic goals that can be positively achieved. Through the exploration of theoretical approaches to leadership and vision, the multifaceted aspects of the marketing vision's 'creative tension' will be evaluated.

The role of reflective practice will then be examined through action modes in marketing research development, whereby 'double-loop' learning is applied to question the underlying assumptions of strategic marketing planning. Chris Argyris (1982, 1985, 1990) developed the term 'double-loop' learning to explain how individuals learn, and that self-realisation or self-actualisation not only helps individuals but also helps the organisation in which they work, leading to how 'loop' learning connects both the organisation and the individual. Nevertheless, barriers to learning in organisations are often complex and interwoven within and across the interactions between managers, leaders, and employees (Kotter, 1990; Senge, 1990).

Chris Argyris (1993) coined the term 'skilled incompetence' to explain why otherwise-effective and intelligent managers and leaders use their highly developed communication skills to consciously or unconsciously suppress positive, constructive attempts to address the problems differently than the way they think fit. 'Skilled incompetence' is

DOI: 10.4324/9781003365136-9

when someone is blind to alternative views other than their own. The difficulty in addressing this complex issue is in part, approached through the concept of double-loop learning. You may recall from Chapters 3 and 7 Argyris and Schön's (1974, 1978) studies of organisations (which they termed 'theory in use'). They researched how managers' behaviour falls under either model I or model II. Within these models, skilled incompetence would fall within model I behaviour, whereby the manager/leader has a very unilateral view of their world. As discussed earlier, individuals employ double-loop learning by utilising reflection and action as a method of learning that goes beyond the simple correction of an error and works to clarify and correct the mental models that resulted in the error(s) in the first place.

An example to illustrate this point is as follows: Two marketing teams are working on the same campaign, where Team A relies on their part for Team B to ensure various products needed are supplied in time. When the products do not arrive, Team A is furious with Team B, and everything from the organisation's perspective goes wrong from then on. The concept of *double-loop learning* as applied here would be to ensure that delays are factored in initially, and the *action* is how they are planned – remember the importance of the critical path methods in project management (Chapter 3)? So both teams would need to consider all the different variables involved in their campaign and plan accordingly. (Remember, too, from project management in Chapter 3, inclement weather and managing risks must be included in the planning time frame!)

## THEORIES OF LEADERSHIP

In the same way as studies of management have grown, so too has research into leadership. Over the past hundred years, different themes of leadership have emerged. Research into leadership has moved from studies of leadership behaviour to how a leader influences an organisation, to personality traits and influence. In the twenty-first century, scholars have explored various approaches to understanding successful leadership. It can simply be stated that a leader is someone who can influence a process in a group or organisation. Leadership, therefore, can be defined as 'a process whereby an individual influences a group of individuals to achieve a common goal' (Northouse, 2019, p. 5).

Leadership is conceptualised as an *effect* rather than a *cause*; leadership development from this perspective consists of using social (relational systems) to help build commitments among members of a community of practice (Day, 2000, p. 583). Leadership is showing the way and helping or inducing others to pursue it. This entails envisioning a desirable future, promoting a clear purpose or mission, maintaining supportive values and intelligent strategies, and empowering and engaging all those involved (Gill, 2011, p. 9). To achieve success in a business, therefore, it can be stated that leadership may be defined by six core themes and practices, as follows:

1. Envisioning a desirable future.
2. Promoting a clear purpose or mission.
3. Maintaining supportive values.

**FIGURE 9.28** Leadership: trust, effort, achievement, motivation.

4. Creating intelligent strategies.
5. Empowering all those concerned.
6. Engaging all those concerned.

(adapted from Gill, 2011)

Of course, leadership is not a moral concept, and leaders are just ordinary individuals, with the same positive and negative traits and flaws as all of us (Kellerman, 2004). Studies of leadership in the military have indicated how much stress is placed on the importance of such factors as facilitating command and control, developing an appropriate strategy, and encouraging ethical conduct, all of which build trust and courage in setting and achieving team goals. In the business sector, leadership texts provide examples of practising executives where case studies are offered, showing brilliant examples of leadership, often referring to strong military leaders, termed 'heroic leaders' – people who turned around, failing organisations (apparently single-handedly, and they took the credit!); but what about all the people who worked on the strategy for change to happen? So what happens when things go wrong? Is it because the strategy is impossible to implement, or is it because the leader is not in touch with the situation, or is it the fault of the employees?

To ensure effective leadership, there must be empowerment and not blame and a practical strategy that is clearly communicated. So a good leader must reflect on their own decisions and actions before they can adopt a strategy of either distributed leadership or shared leadership (Rizvi, 2023). *Distributed leadership* is one where leadership, responsibilities, and decision-making are divided up among team members, while *shared leadership*, on the other hand, is where all members of a team share equally in the three aforementioned tasks, through a collective approach; either of these strategies can encourage advantageous cooperation and team spirit. The success of either of these strategies is of course dependent upon the organisational hierarchy and whether or not it can be flexible, or whether the very nature of the business means that decision-making and leadership have to be 'top-down' and hierarchical, as is the case in most government departments; consequently, governments throughout the world face challenges to leadership at all levels.

Politicians' leadership skills are related to how effective they are at implementing their governments' policies. Kavanagh (1990) refers to political leaders as either reconcilers or mobilisers, with examples from political leaders of the past such as Lloyd George, Joseph Chamberlain, and Tony Benn, who were all primarily concerned with radical change through achieving policy goals rather than reconciliation of differences. In contrast, Kavanagh (1990) argued, mobilisers may be transformational leaders who emerge out of dissatisfaction or crisis, such as the late Winston Churchill in the UK (Kavanagh, 1990). Politicians' leadership skills throughout the globe were tested to the hilt when the Covid-19 pandemic spread across the globe (WHO, 2023). The speed of the virus spread meant politicians' need for strong leadership skills was critical in gaining data from scientists and health professionals on how best to respond and act. Hope Hailey and Jacobs (2022) researched the impact of the pandemic through the eyes of over 150 leaders, and their findings showed that living through the experience of the pandemic had changed leadership experience. Hope Hailey and Jacobs (2022, p. 4) said that Covid-19 'disrupted leaders on every level, making them re-examine their assumptions about their organisation's purpose and place in society. . . . [I]t impacted their perceptions and actions around responsible business, and their leadership attitudes and practices'. In their research, Hope Hailey and Jacobs (2022) designed their questions on Pless et al.'s (2022) model of four types of leadership orientations, as follows:

1. Idealist (high accountability, narrow focus)
2. Integrator (high accountability, broad focus)
3. Traditional economist (low accountability, narrow focus)
4. Opportunity seeker (low accountability, broad focus)

Depending on which orientation the leader aligns with, as noted, influences the impact on their stakeholder groups; however, this was all thrown into turmoil during the leaders' need to respond to the challenges the pandemic presented. There was an immediate need for all leaders, regardless of their views and orientation to leadership, to increase accountability around responsible business, and the pandemic emphasised the interconnected nature of business and society. As noted by Hope Hailey and Jacobs (2022, p. 30), 'the world has shifted, not just because of Covid-19, but because this disruption has had a domino effect, changing work and personal lives for leaders and "followers" alike; this disruption has elevated the demands for new forms of responsible leadership'.

The Covid-19 pandemic also emphasised the challenges in successfully responding to climate change. Responsible leadership is necessary in terms of the challenges faced in dealing with changes to the climate, 'as hard-won compromises achieved at COP26 cast doubts on whether our leaders have been bold enough in their agreement' (Levin and De

Ganay, 2021). Marketing can contribute to positive impacts on the climate as leaders in marketing promote 'climate-friendly' business behaviours and products.

In terms of a marketing career, a good leader is therefore responsible in their actions and could be described in terms such as: 'He/she really understood the essence of the product and led a brilliant marketing campaign.' To describe leadership in these terms would be taking a trait perspective, suggesting that some individuals have certain characteristics or qualities that allow them to stand out within a group. Whereas from a process perspective leadership is 'a phenomenon that resides in the context of the interactions between leaders and followers and makes leadership available to everyone' (Northouse, 2019, p. 7).

Whether it was a business organisation or a military unit, traditional studies of leadership focused on what it meant to be outstanding, with personality traits such as intelligence, self-confidence, integrity, and determination (Northouse, 2019) considered essential for leaders. Contemporary and future studies of leadership have become complex and explore the fusion of leadership from within cross-cultural and interdisciplinary contexts. Hence, research into leadership may take a psychological or sociological stance (Schedlitzki and Edwards, 2018). Psychodynamic theories explore the leader–member exchange (LMX) models, whereby leaders provide direction and guidance through influence permitted by members, termed exchange theory or vertical dyad linkage theory, which focuses on the characteristics of leaders, individual followers, and the relationship between the two. However, this is often criticised as not being fair to all employees (Northouse, 2019). In a similar way, transactional theories of leadership involve transaction or exchange between leaders and followers, the management of which is by exception and could be passive or active (Byrd and Sparkman, 2022). Objectives and performance standards will be set, and the transactional leader will ensure managers enforce the rules and standards. In contrast, transformational leadership, from the seminal work of McGregor-Burns (1978), occurs when both leaders and followers help each other by elevating their respective morale and motivation. Further psychological analysis, however, such as the work of Jean Lipman-Blumen (2005), shows how some leaders can become too self-serving and become 'toxic' to the organisation and its purpose. This is when leaders first charm and then manipulate, mistreat, weaken, and eventually devastate their followers, in what Lipman-Blumen (2005) stated was because human beings can often be susceptible to toxic leadership through a process of 'transference'. Leaders cannot exist without followers, and toxic leadership can be devastating to the morale and motivation of those who are being led.

A classic example of toxic leadership is the case of the collapse of the Enron Corporation (2001); while the company enjoyed initial market success, this covered up internal dishonesty and intimidation, described by Cross (2018, p. 15) as 'disingenuous and self-serving leadership'. Promoting the right people into leadership positions shapes the strategy and organisational climate for years. When leaders are chosen, there is the least opportunity for trial-and-error learning, while business cycles are hard to see, and thus to learn from them, as often these cycles don't last longer than a year or two. It may not be until the leader of the organisation has left or been replaced before the true impact of their influence/strategy can be known (Senge, 1990, p. 23). In her work, Barbara Tuchman (1984) explored the 'darker side' of leadership. She looked back in history to study leadership by tyranny or oppression, excessive ambition, incompetence or decadence, or by folly or perversity. Self-interest is whatever is conducive to the welfare of the body being governed; folly is a leadership policy that, in these terms, is clearly counter-productive (Tuchman, 1984).

From a leadership perspective, therefore, all different types of organisations have tried a number of approaches to ensure their employees feel included; so from these leadership studies, the concept of 'inclusive leadership' has emerged. In the healthcare sector, Nembhard and Edmondson (2006) were among the first researchers to look more closely at how the actions of leaders were critical to employees' sense of value. While an effective leader can be called *transformational*, being totally inclusive in leadership style can be seen as more complex and multifaceted. Studies of inclusive leadership and communicating the company's vision have therefore explored the complexity of how leaders can nurture employees' sense of belonging and uniqueness (Brewer, 1991). As observed by Argyris (1990) in his research into reflection's role in double-loop learning, an inclusive leadership approach is very important, and perhaps more so in the creative industries, simply because of the nature of subjective expression in creativity. Employees must feel secure to be able to suggest ideas close to their heart. As Groves and Feyerherm (2022, p. 978), however, argue in their paper on leadership development, the challenges presented to organisations today, through fast-changing technologies, 'environmental complexity, and volatility', mean there needs to be new leadership models devised. Researching the healthcare sector in the USA, they found that leaders with strong collaborative skills who are emerging as possible leaders in an organisation must have strategic insight and be comfortable with ambiguity. In the modern world, other scholars argue that as well as knowing how best to be able to work inclusively with change, a leader needs to be responsible and compassionate. As the world has attempted to respond to the challenges of climate change, civil disruption in many regions, along with the recent pandemic, has highlighted the need for compassion as an essential component of successful leadership if leaders of the future are to be able to navigate through the complexity and uncertainty of business and society (Haskins et al., 2018).

Whatever the nature of the leader, they must be capable; therefore, the ability to engage in reflection on all aspects of behaviour is critical in order to learn to develop the personality characteristics described by Finkelstein et al. (2007) as occurring across five areas, as follows:

1. Positive – ability to enable transformation.
2. Negative – ability to deal with negative situations (people and context).
3. Conceptual – ability to master systems.
4. Creative – ability to 'think outside the box'.
5. Relational – ability to relate and build trust.

## LEADING MARKETING TEAMS – MANAGING AND DIRECTING CREATIVE TENSION

Leading marketing teams and managing and directing creative tension is, therefore, a key challenge in competitive environments nowadays. As discussed in Chapter 3, sustainability is key to a company adapting to quickly changing environments that the modern world presents, as outlined by Groves and Feyerhem's (2022) in their research into 'developing a leadership potential model for the new era of work and organizations'. Here are some examples of views of leadership from different business areas.

## STUDIES OF LEADERSHIP IN PRACTICE

### CASE STUDY 9.1

*Peter Henry and John Husband*

Peter Henry, together with John Husband, started '*totrain*' in 1999, and the business has been delivering top-quality training solutions to the food industry ever since. With many international and SME clients, *totrain* provides food industry–specific training solutions that meet the needs of each organisation through digital, traditional, and blended methods. Peter Henry (2023) believes team building through motivation and positive support is critical for a successful business, be it a very large or a small organisation. He said that 'effective leadership is creating positive change by inspiring and motivating your teams, and establishing an environment where colleagues enjoy their roles and responsibilities and strive to perform at their highest capability'.

## LEADERSHIP AND MARKETING – RESEARCH INTO THE CULTURAL ASPECTS OF FOOD SAFETY COMPLIANCE

### CASE STUDY 9.2

*Associate Professor Derek Watson*

Associate Professor Derek Watson's research examines the impact of knowledge exchange on practice and food safety cultural compliance. He has worked with a number of companies across the globe in various locations from Beijing to Panama. His research explores how different cultures endeavour to comply with both food safety regulations and certification bodies, such as the British Standards Institute and the British Retail Consortium Global Standards. The golden thread running through most organisations is that they need to demonstrate compliance with industrial standards in order to strengthen their marketing brand both domestically and in the international markets. To do this, some organisations often fail to effectively market their food safety compliance internally to their existing employees, which subsequently hinders any external marketing campaign. A company's marketing brand can take many years to establish but can be lost overnight, often due to a flaw in leadership in failing to appreciate the importance in nurturing a proactive culture, which very much includes marketing and effective marketing communications.

## LEADERSHIP AND MANAGEMENT IN HUMAN RESOURCE MANAGEMENT

### CASE STUDY 9.3

*Jane Bell*

Jane Bell is the human resources business partner at the University of Sunderland. She has worked in HRM for over 20 years and has seen considerable changes in the importance of the role of human resources in recruiting and managing staff. Part of this role is working closely with managers in the business school; Jane says that the key issues facing HRM is creating the right balance of a number of factors, such as being a strategic partner, creating equitable environments, finding good leaders, attracting and retaining talent, creating job satisfaction, and nurturing engagement in the workplace (particularly post-Covid). She said that:

> Being a leader is no mean feat; it never has been and will continue to be the toughest role in a business. Despite the ever-changing landscape around leaders, from technology to employment law, I believe there is one important factor that has remained the most important: 'mindset'. Although this translates into skills which can be learned, my view is more effectively that it begins with a 'growth mindset', as described by Dr Carol Dweck (2012).
>
> I often acknowledge to leaders that it is very lonely the further to the top they get! So having a growth mindset enables a tunnel out of issues, and a tunnel into opportunities. I believe the result of adopting a growth mindset is then the ability to learn skills needed at whichever point in time. This growth mindset enables resilience and persistence, and I typically see skills being applied successfully by leaders with growth mindsets, such as the ability to be authentic, to create a culture of learning, to facilitate role-modelling, to be able to give clear direction and communication, to appreciate diversity, to trust their staff, and finally, to be a leader who is unafraid to make the right decisions no matter how tough.
>
> A leader with a fixed mindset obsesses about the end result with a fixed point in time and doesn't allow for other factors to be at play. They are

disappointed in failure, they prioritise presenteeism, while they are frustrated and become disillusioned if they are not considered the best at what they do. This leader may succeed for a short period of time, but their success as a leader in the longer term will be limited.

Leaders with growth mindsets can adapt themselves and are continuously learning and therefore create a nurturing wake behind them: a culture of continuous growth which is hugely motivating and empowering for staff. During the Covid pandemic, we saw leaders who made very, very tough decisions, almost sometimes on a daily basis, and it was the leaders with the growth mindsets that were not looking at the end result but turning up every day with their growth mindset and acknowledging the effort along the way.

## TASKS

**Task 1.** Think of a leader you admire. What personal qualities do they have? Make a note of them.

**Task 2.** Review the list you have written, then referring to Finkelstein et al.'s (2007) list of characteristics across the five areas, try to write examples alongside each area:

1. Positive – ability to enable transformation.
2. Negative – ability to deal with negative situations (people and context).
3. Conceptual – ability to master systems.
4. Creative – ability to 'think outside the box'.
5. Relational – ability to relate and build trust.

**Task 3.** Reflect back on the knowledge and skills you wrote in the tasks in the previous chapters; what have you learned about yourself, and what do you intend to work on to become a good leader in marketing?

Suggested possible responses are in Chapter 10.

## SUMMARY OF THE CHAPTER

In this chapter, the importance of personal reflection in marketing was discussed within the context of a number of theoretical approaches to leadership and team development. The chapter concluded with an invitation to examine how the qualities of effective leaders may be learned.

The next chapter draws together the topics explored in the book and provides the suggested responses to the tasks.

## REFERENCES

Argyris, C. (1982) *Reasoning, Learning, and Action: Individual and Organizational*. San Francisco: Jossey-Bass.

Argyris, C. (1985) *Strategy, Change and Defensive Routines*. London: Pitman.

Argyris, C. (1990) *Overcoming Organisational Defences*. New York: Prentice Hall.

Argyris, C. (1993) *Knowledge for Action: A Guide to Overcoming Barriers to Organizational Change*. San Francisco: Jossey-Bass.

Argyris, C. and Schön, D.A. (1974) *Theory in Practice: Increasing Professional Effectiveness*. San Francisco: Jossey-Bass.

Argyris, C. and Schön, D.A. (1978) *Organisational Learning: A Theory of Action Perspective*. Wokingham: Addison Wesley.

Bartlett, C. and Ghoshal, S. (2002) Building competitive advantage through people. *MIT Sloan Management Review*, 43(2), 34–41.

Brewer, M.B. (1991) The social self: On being the same and different at the same time. *Personality and Social Psychology Bulletin*, 17, 475–482.

Byrd, M. and Sparkman, T.E. (2022) Reconciling the business case and the social justice case for diversity: A model of human relations. *Journal of Human Resources Development Review*, 21(1), 75–100. https://doi.org/10.1177/15344843211072356.

Cross, S.E. (2018) What kind of leader do you want to be? *IEEE Engineering Management Review*, 46(3), 14–15.

Day, D.V. (2000) Leadership development: A review in context. *Leadership Quarterly*, 11, 581–613.

Dweck, C. (2012) *Mindset. How you can fulfil your potential*. New York: Ballantine Books.

Employment Law: Contract. (2023) Available from: www.gov.uk/employment-contracts-and-conditions.

Finkelstein, S., Harvey, C. and Thomas, L. (2007) *Breakout Strategy: Meeting the Challenge of Double-Digit Growth*. New York: McGraw-Hill.

Gill, R. (2011) *Theory and Practice of Leadership*. London: Sage.

Groves, K.S. and Feyerhem, A.E. (2022) Developing a leadership potential model for the new era of work and organizations. *Leadership & Organization Development Journal*, 43(6), 978–998. DOI: 10.1108/LODJ-06–2021–0258.

Haskins, G., Thomas, M. and Johri, L. (Eds.). (2018) *Kindness in Leadership*. London: Routledge.

Henry, P. and Husband, J. (2023) *Totrain's* website is available from: Home – totrain.

Hope Hailey, V. and Jacobs, K. (2022) *Responsible Business Through Crisis: Has COVID-19 Changed Leadership Forever?* London: Chartered Institute of Personnel and Development. Available from: www.cipd.co.uk/Images/responsible-business-crisis-1_tcm18-112209.pdf.

Kavanagh, D. (1990) *British Politics: Continuities and Change*. 2nd Edition. Oxford: Oxford University Press.

Kellerman, B. (2004) Leadership: Warts and all. *Harvard Business Review*, January 40–45.

Kotter, J.P. (1990) *A Force for Change: How Leadership Differs from Management*. New York: Free Press.

Levin, M. and De Ganay, G. (2021) *Why female leadership is crucial to tackle climate change* | *World Economic Forum*. Available from: (weforum.org) (Accessed 12 February 2023).

Lipman-Blumen, J. (2005) *The Allure of Toxic Leaders*. New York: Oxford University Press.

McGregor-Burns, J. (1978) *Leadership*. New York: Harper & Row.

Nembhard, I.M. and Edmondson, A.C. (2006) Making it safe: The effects of leader inclusiveness and professional status on psychological safety and improvement efforts in health care teams. *Journal of Organizational Behaviour*, 27, 941–966.

Northouse, P.G. (2019) *Leadership, Theory and Practice*. 8th Edition. Thousand Oaks, CA: Sage.

Pless, N., Maak, T. and Waldman, D. (2022) Different approaches toward doing the right thing: Mapping the responsibility orientation of leaders. In N. Pless and T. Maak (Eds.), *Responsible Leadership*. 2nd Edition. London: Routledge.

Rizvi, H. (2023) *Horizontal Leadership*. Available from his blog article: https://hidaya-trizvi.com/distributed-leadership-vs . . . (Accessed 22 February 2023).

Schedlitzki, D. and Edwards, G. (2018) *Studying Leadership. Traditional and Critical Approaches*. 2nd Edition. London: Sage.

Senge, P.M. (1990) *The Fifth Discipline. The Art & Practice of the Learning Organisation*. London: Random House.

Tuchman, B.W. (1984) *The March of Folly from Troy to Vietnam*. London: Abacus.

Watson, D., Nyarugwe, S.P., Hogg, R., Griffith, C., Luning, P. and Pandi, S. (2022) The exotropia food safety cultural conundrum? A case study of a UK fish high-risk processing company. *Food Control Journal*, 131, 108431. ISSN 0956–7135. https://doi.org/10.1016/j.foodcont.2021.108431.

World Health Organisation. (2023) *WHO Coronavirus (COVID-19) Dashboard* | WHO Coronavirus (COVID-19) Dashboard with Vaccination Data.

## RECOMMENDED FURTHER READING:-

Covey, S. (1989) *Seven Habits of Highly Effective People*. New York: Simon & Schuster.

*Authors' Comment:* Very clear and accessible text on how leaders begin their journey to success in their profession and/or organisation.

Cross, S.E. (2018) What kind of leader do you want to be? *IEEE Engineering Management Review*, 46(3), 14–15.

*Authors' Comment:* Cross shows how things can go terribly wrong when the morals of the leaders are questionable.

Haskins, G., Thomas, M. and Johri, L. (Eds.). (2018) *Kindness in Leadership*. London Routledge.

*Authors' Comment:* Very thoughtful and insightful and a must read for any new manager.

Northouse, P.G. (2019) *Leadership, Theory and Practice*. 8th Edition. Thousand Oaks, CA: Sage.

*Authors' Comment:* A very good introduction to all aspects of leadership with clear explanations of developments in theories of leadership.

Schedlitzki, D. and Edwards, G. (2018) *Studying Leadership. Traditional and Critical Approaches*. 2nd Edition. London: Sage.

*Authors' Comment:* Clear and easy to read about how research into leadership has progressed.

Senge, P.M. (1990) *The Fifth Discipline. The Art & Practice of the Learning Organisation*. London: Random House.

*Authors' Comment:* Senge shows how learning and adapting to change is critical for any organisation to prosper.

Tuchman, B.W. (1984) *The March of Folly from Troy to Vietnam*. London: Abacus.

*Authors' Comment:* Easy to read and offers insight into errors of judgement and their tragic consequences.

## CHAPTER 10

# Marketing in industry 5.0

## SYNOPSIS AND LEARNING OUTCOMES

At the end of this chapter, successful students will be able to do the following:

1.  Demonstrate an understanding of the challenges of sustainability.
2.  Explain the impact and issues in AI and digital technology.
3.  Appreciate the possible futures of marketing in organisations.

## INTRODUCTION

Marketing is a fast-changing world, and advancements in technology mean the pace of change is even quicker. In this book, we have examined how marketing has evolved to become a specialised area of work, providing a wide range of employment and research opportunities. The chapter case studies provide illustrations of what it is to work in marketing. The tasks throughout the book provide an opportunity for the application of understanding and reflection, with suggested responses offered for guidance in Chapter 10.

The book is in two sections. Section 1 presented the context of marketing, starting with an overview of how marketing has developed over the past two decades. While technology and digital resources are critical to promote and evaluate marketing, there are many more facets to successful marketing, and these were discussed in the first section of the book. Professional practitioners' and academics' perspectives are fundamental to fully articulate marketing practice, and the viewpoints in the case studies in Section 1 highlight the skills and knowledge required to succeed in marketing. Section 2 then shows how to apply the theories of management and leadership in marketing to practice and then relate this knowledge to an individual's transferable skills and professional development. The content of the chapters is summarised next.

In Chapters 1 and 2, we reviewed how marketing is defined and then examined how industry and its relationships with developing technological aspects not only impacts on but also disrupts marketing. We then discussed the integrated influences on the development

DOI: 10.4324/9781003365136-10

**FIGURE 10.29** The Earth environment: mountains and lakes.

of marketing, resulting from the explosion of data, the spread of social media, the shifting consumer demographics, and the opportunities and challenges presented in the proliferation of digital marketing channels.

In Chapter 3, we examined the development and impact of theories of management and leadership and showed how they have been applied in marketing across all sectors of society and business. We then presented a discussion of the skills and knowledge required for a marketing career in Chapters 4 and 5; this was underpinned by case studies from practitioners and academics which presented the diversity of different career journeys. The acquisition of how professional identity is developed was then explored in Chapter 6, followed by insights into self-management in marketing in Chapter 7. Managing others, being a leader, and the importance of learning from reflection were then examined in Chapters 8 and 9, with the conclusion and suggested responses to the tasks concluding the book.

## WHAT DO CURRENT MARKETERS DO, AND WHAT DOES THE FUTURE OF MARKETING HOLD?

Throughout the book, we examined the impact of social media and showed why marketers need to know how and why people use the Internet, social media, and all digital sources. Future marketers must ensure they keep up to date with learning how to apply the formal standards of digital language alongside the latest technologies. The role of public relations in managing the image of a company has grown in importance, particularly in terms of ensuring sustainability in marketing practice. Equally, the communication process and how it has evolved on an international and global level will also increase in importance. Marketers must consider different countries, language differences, symbols and religion, values, and beliefs and decide whether or not to standardise or adapt a product or service to a local situation. Historical research into marketing shows how it has contributed to our personal and social identities, and so the study of the language of marketing provides insight into how societal values have developed and changed perspective over the past decades.

The study of marketing as a discipline has evolved over the decades to embrace the advancement of marketing orientation strategies, relationship marketing and brand equity, and so on. Developed from the work of Wilkie and Moore (2003) on 'four eras of marketing thought', Hunt (2018) argued for further research into Era V, which is the current stage of marketing today. Era V marketing strategies mean increasing the influence of strategic marketing, whereby artificial intelligence (AI) and digital technologies will embrace virtual reality to create more personalised marketing platforms. The nature of language discourse and influence in marketing terms has thus also come to the fore in advertising and product promotion. To meet current and future challenges, therefore, marketers need to be more critical scholars.

Current issues facing chief marketing officers (CMOs) include how best to market brands in the aftermath of the global pandemic. Denlinger and Seidenschwarz's (2023) findings from their interviews with 20 CMOs across the globe showed that investing in marketing in a downturn could contribute to future growth, so rather than cutting costs with their marketing, CMOs were prioritising three strategies:

### 1. Accelerating the move to new digital technologies or platforms.

In previous chapters, we have shown how trends in marketing have moved to more personalised customer interactions through digital platforms, and some marketers have prioritised artificial intelligence (AI) and analytics to help provide a better experience for the customer. The design of accessible platforms means that customers are encouraged to buy the product or service.

### 2. Expanding into new markets, segments, or geographies.

The advanced technology in digital marketing provides opportunities through 'microsegmentation' and the precision of data to help reach the target customers.

### 3. Implementing systems or algorithms to enhance customer personalisation.

New platform advancements in digital technology make it possible to integrate information gathered from a wide range of sources; 'the evolution in personalization brings data directly to the marketer' (Denlinger and Seidenschwarz, 2023, p. 1).

While there is a current and future need for marketers to keep up to date with digital technologies, the principles of marketing remain. That is, to provide quality products and services to customers in an ethical and responsible manner. The jobs that people hold in marketing today will be very different in ten years' time – what does the future hold? We propose that the impact and integration of digital/interactive technologies will increase and bring many opportunities and challenges. Artificial intelligence and intelligent machines and robots have been utilised in business for many years, for example, in manufacturing and production. Robots, termed 'bots', have now been utilised in consumer markets, and these are predicted to increase in the future. Bots are automated programs that perform specific commands when instructed (as in robots); examples can be found in chat room hosts who greet customers and 'spiders' that access websites to retrieve their content for search engine indexes (Baines and Fill, 2014, p. 706). Over the past decade, the use and range of AI and bots have increased dramatically, and this is predicted to increase.

Marr (2022) stated that AI is currently used extensively in marketing, as there are so many AI features that are all used unconsciously, such as social and search engine advertising solutions, but in the future, as AI advances, AI will be used more robustly. For example, to analyse data to predict how best to market a product to maximise efficiency. Marr (2022) said that 'a McKinsey study found that, along with sales, it is the single business function where it will have the most financial impact'. This means that if you're a marketer and you're not using AI, you're missing out on the benefits of what is possibly the most transformational technology. More advanced applications are emerging, such as ChatGPT.

Vallance (2022) reported on the introduction of a new artificial intelligence system called ChatGPT that was released in December 2022 by OpenAI, an artificial intelligence research firm. GPT is an acronym which stands for Generative Pre-Trained Transformer. ChatGPT is programmed to offer human-like answers to questions.

Vallance asked the ChatGPT a few questions, such as, 'Did it think AI would take jobs from human writers? No – it argued that AI systems like me can help writers by providing suggestions and ideas, but ultimately it is up to the human writer to create a final product.' ChatGPT learns from human interactions, and so development in AI and applications will undoubtedly grow in the next decade, and as Sam Altman, OpenAI Chief Executive, is quoted as saying in Vallance's (2022) article, 'AI has a long way to go, and big ideas yet to discover. We will stumble along the way, and learn a lot from contact with reality'.

Using AI in bots such as ChatGPT continues to stir debate, especially around the ethics of their use. Research by Tóth et al. (2022), however, argues that there must be an accountability framework to ensure that the organisations' use of AI is ethical at all times. The accountability framework is developed within normal business ethics around four clusters, as follows:

1. *Supererogatory.* Actions represent a positive extra mile from what is expected morally.

2. *Illegal.* Any action that is against laws and regulations.

3. *Immoral.* Any action that only reaches the legal threshold's bare minimum.

4. *Permissible.* Actions not requiring explanations of putative fairness or appropriateness.

Ethical evaluations should show the locus of morality, that is, the level of autonomy to choose an ethical course of action, and moral intensity, the potential consequences of the use of AI robots.

The four clusters of accountability are:

1. *Professional norms.* Whereby AI robots are used for small tasks, such as cleaning, and robot design experts take most responsibility.

2. *Business responsibility.* Whereby AI robots are used for difficult but basic tasks, for example, mining. In this cluster, a wider group of organisations must be responsible for the AI robots.

3. *Inter-institutional normativity.* AI robots may make decisions such as in healthcare settings or crime fighting. In this cluster, regulatory bodies and governments must set specific guidelines.

4. *Supra-territorial regulations.* AI robots are used on a global level, such as the military or driverless cars. In this cluster, there is a need for inter-agency accountability, and this requires much closer interrogation of how accountability can be maintained.

Tóth et al. (2022) emphasised the importance of implementing and evaluating the use of AI robots against this ethical framework. They also highlighted the fact that humans control what/how the AI robots can learn and unlearn.

Ethics or moral principles are critical to responsible marketing, not just to the responsible use of AI robots. Professional marketing organisations adhere to a code of conduct as identified by the Chartered Institute of Marketing (2020). The CIM Code of Conduct (2020) includes a requirement for its members to demonstrate integrity and to avoid the dissemination of false or misleading information.

Along with ethical practice, corporate social responsibility has increased in importance, particularly in business-to-business marketing, whereby transactions cross the globe.

## BUSINESS-TO-BUSINESS MARKETING

Business-to-business marketing is not as transparent as consumer marketing, but it is a huge part of business transactions. It is termed the business market and business-to-business (B2B) and means the buying and selling of products and services between one company and another (Kotler and Armstrong, 2020). B2B is a far larger market than consumer markets. For example, if you consider major construction projects such as buildings or roads, there are many different types and sizes of organisations that will be involved. A key part of B2B is sustainable relationships, and this is increasingly important in relation to the need for ethical transactions and corporate social responsibility.

Environmentalism started with organised groups such as Greenpeace and related support groups in the 1960s and 1970s, and they started to raise awareness of how the ecosystem was damaged by business and consumer behaviour. When they started in 1971, the first major campaign is recorded by Greenpeace (2023) as follows:

Greenpeace was founded in 1971 by a small group of concerned individuals, who set sail to Amchitka island off the coast of Alaska to try and stop a US nuclear weapons test. Their old fishing boat was called 'The Greenpeace'. Today, Greenpeace is present in over 40 countries around the world. Our movement is growing every day and our commitment to realising our vision is as strong as ever.

We find ourselves at a pivotal point in human history now. Climate change is rapidly accelerating and we are feeling the effects of it ever more – in the changes to our air, sea levels and more extreme weather events. The need to act to protect our planet has never been so urgent, yet governments and corporations are still dragging their feet. Our mission is to promote radical changes and new solutions to the ways we live on this planet so that we can all call it home for generations to come.

Greenpeace (2023) has embraced the latest digital technologies to continue to spread awareness of environmental issues throughout the world. The marketing of their concerns is now professionally organised, and they actively promote non-violent action in any of their protests. Their investigations endeavour to publish accurate factual studies that are researched utilising a variety of methods, such as fieldwork, satellite imagery, business and financial analysis, and working with whistle-blowers. For example, their investigations led to improvements in waste disposal and industrial fishing (Unearthed, 2023). Other organisations, such as the Global Environment Facility, also work to address negative impact on the ecosystem. The Global Environment Facility (GEF) raises funds to support developing countries' work to address the world's urgent environmental issues over five focal areas: 'biodiversity loss, chemicals and waste, climate change, international waters and land degradation – and take an integrated approach to support more sustainable food systems, forest management and cities' (GEF, 2023).

In response to environmental concerns raised in the 1970s and 1980s, governments throughout the globe have passed laws and regulations governing industrial practices that impact on the environment. After the oil crises in 1973, ministers from Britain, the United State, France, Japan, and West Germany (as it was at that time) met informally to work on major global issues. These meetings then continued, and the 2015 Paris Agreement to limit global emissions was formed. The group of ministers has now grown to seven, and their meetings are called G7 Summit, with the members now being the United Kingdom, the United States of America, Canada, France, Germany, Italy, and Japan. Other countries are also invited to these meetings. The 2023 G7 summit is scheduled to take place from May 19 to 21 in Hiroshima, Japan (G7, 2023).

The issues raised by environmental movements have now converged to move from protests to prevention, with more regulation to support responsible and sustainable business and lifestyles. All parts of marketing communications must therefore represent the changes required in business to ensure sustainable and responsible practice. The future of global marketing, therefore, is a growth in narrative and non-verbal messaging, whereby impact and responsibility are ecological, 'green', and sustainable (Percy, 2023; Quesenberry and Coolsen, 2023). The following case study highlights how local businesses started to market sustainability by encouraging their employees to avoid driving their cars to work and look to alternative methods, such as walking, cycling, or public transport.

## CASE STUDY 10.1

*Dr Derek Watson*

### Marketing the business clinic and a 'green' campaign

Developing graduates' employment skills are at the heart of the current provision for a university education, and many universities have professional business-to-business and/or enterprise and innovation departments to work closely with local employers. As part of these initiatives to embed employment skills in the curriculum, research was conducted to raise awareness of how students can work on live projects with businesses. Dr Derek Watson led a project to research how students could work with local businesses on live projects. The skills students were to develop were to be set against the 'understanding, skills, efficacy and metacognition model' (USEM) developed by Knight and Yorke (2003). These skills are part of the knowledge and skills needed in the fast-changing digital marketing required by businesses today (CIM, 2023).

Dr Derek Watson (2023) said:

> I am currently working with local businesses to raise awareness of how our students can work with them on live projects, and of course, many of our students start up their own businesses. I have built a strong relationship with many of our local employers over the past ten years, and we regularly receive enquiries for marketing projects that now go to the Marketing Hub for processing. The aim of one of the initial projects a few years ago was to help students develop their understanding of business and marketing, through working with local employers. The first year involved a team of academic staff and students working together to see what could be achieved. It started with a proposal to management to introduce a student-led business clinic. The venture was approved, and finance raised through grants interest there could be in the locality, and 2,000 flyers detailing the plans for the business clinic were sent out both electronically and by post to sole traders, small and medium enterprises (on average 50 employees), and larger international companies with offices in the region.
>
> While the initial response rate was disappointing at less than 8%, this changed dramatically, and a further 160 companies were then represented at a series of business breakfasts and seminars that were organised by students, assisted by academic staff. From these events and some further related networking, the first phase concentrated on establishing the need for a business clinic and clarifying what sort of projects may emerge. Ten academic staff working with students formed four focus groups to divide the employers' needs/queries into four different sectors: management, innovation and enterprise, supply chain operations, and marketing.

The issues around possible projects that emerged from the business awareness sessions were grouped across four different areas of business: management, innovation and enterprise, supply chain operations, and marketing. The issues in marketing included companies' queries about innovation, digital marketing, and how they can be competitive through improvements in their marketing strategies.

One of the marketing projects was for a local hospital. The task was for students to research how to encourage staff to find alternative means of transport to get to work rather than use their cars. The second task was then to create a 'green' advertising campaign. Firstly, students had to conduct the research and report on their findings, and secondly, they had to design a 'green campaign' to encourage staff not to use their cars to go into work. Twelve teams of students were invited to research what factors prevented the hospital's 1,300 staff from walking, cycling, or using public transport rather than their own cars to get to work. Mentored by an academic member of staff, 84 postgraduate students formed 12 teams of seven members to conduct the research. They designed questionnaires and conducted interviews with the hospital staff, presenting their findings in a report to the hospital's senior management team.

The students were then asked to design a logo for the 'green campaign'. This project involved the 84 postgraduate students, who were subsequently joined by a further group of 17 students who expressed an interest in the design of the campaign logo. The hospital's senior management team awarded a cash prize of £600 to the winning team.

The senior managers were pleased with the students' work, and an HR manager commented:

We were initially quite apprehensive as, normally, we seek external commercial support; however, the students delivered, and their professionalism, competence, and creativity were exceptional. We will certainly be utilising students in future projects and feel that the students also benefited in terms of employability.

Another NHS manager said '[t]he students demonstrated good organisational skills throughout the exercise; it was quite evident and reassuring that their academic programmes had provided the students key skills and competencies to work as a team and produce excellent results'.

Students said they enjoyed the real projects but noted how they underestimated the time and commitment. This is where we continue to stress the need for students to learn basic marketing planning, and working together with local businesses provides the opportunity for students to gain confidence as they can see what works and what does not.

Detailed findings of the project were reported in Watson and Barkas (2018).

# RESPONSES TO THE CHAPTER TASKS

## Chapter 1

### *Task 1.1*

Create your own definition of marketing.

Here it is likely that you have considered the different definitions put forward in this book and perhaps researched a few more. Your definition should be influenced by your own perspective and experiences of marketing.

### *Task 1.2*

Go back to your own definition of marketing. How does it compare to the preceding definitions? Note the similarities or 'golden threads' of marketing. Now think about all the marketing terms and words you have read.

It is good to appreciate academic and practitioner viewpoints. There are synergies or 'golden threads'. For instance, you might consider the following to be examples:

- Customers
- Stakeholders
- Consumers
- Needs
- Wants
- Value
- Research and identification
- Data-informed decision-making
- Target markets
- Exchange
- Actions
- Orientation
- Process
- Planning and management

There are, of course, others. Please read around the subject of marketing. It is an interesting, challenging, and constantly changing subject with many nuances and perspectives.

### *Task 1.3*

Think of a name for the vegetarian shop and café.

Responses will show awareness of the issues. For example, checking the name is not already taken. In the UK, this would be through Companies House. It is important to make sure the chosen name is not offensive when translated into another language. The letters for 'vegetarian shop and café' (VSC) may stand for something inappropriate in another language.

Consideration should be given to the association with the name. For example, is the choice of word customer-centric, meaning, that the customer could easily associate the name with the shop and the café? This is not always critical, but it should be memorable rather than obscure. For example, Bill Gates's operating system is called Windows, and Steve Job chose the name Apple for the computer.

The name should have longevity – is the name popular now but would be out of fashion in a couple of years? Association with colours, fruit, or vegetables may be appealing in the short-term, but would they last? This is not an easy task at all!

## Chapter 2

### Task 2.1

Imagine you are working as a marketing manager in your selected industry. Identify the key threats and opportunities.

Every answer will be different here; however, you should have utilised PESTLE to help you. In addition to this, you will have focused on what is likely to have a negative or positive impact on your target market. You should have considered things such as the size of your market and whether it is growing or shrinking, whether it is still accessible, and whether there are any opportunities or threats in the way you may reach and serve it. What are you competitors doing? What about your partners and suppliers? Trends in marketing, such as digital, may, for instance, be impacting on consumer behaviour.

### Task 2.2

Research what is meant by Industry 5.0 and consider how this might impact on those working in marketing.

You should research Industry 5.0 and apply it to the marketing industry.

A brief insight from Europa (2023) is provided here, but please do read around the subject Industry 5.0 (europa.eu).

European industry is a key driver in the economic and societal transitions that we are currently undergoing. In order to remain the engine of prosperity, industry must lead the digital and green transitions. This approach provides a vison of industry that aims beyond efficiency and productivity as the sole goals and reinforces the role and the contribution of industry to society. It places the well-being of the worker at the centre of the production process and uses new technologies to provide prosperity beyond jobs and growth while respecting the production limits of the planet. It complements the existing 'Industry 4.0' approach by specifically putting research and innovation at the service of the transition to a sustainable, human-centric, and resilient European industry.

### Why Industry 5.0?

Industries can play an active role in providing solutions to challenges for society, including the preservation of resources, climate change, and social stability. The industry of the future approach brings benefits for industry, for workers, and for society. It empowers workers as well as addresses the evolving skills and training needs of employees. It increases the competitiveness of industry and helps attract the best talents.

It is good for our planet as it favours circular production models and supports technologies that make the use of natural resources more efficient. Revising existing value chains and energy consumption practices can also make industries more resilient against external shocks, such as the Covid-19 crisis.

Elements related to the future of industry are already part of major commission policy initiatives:

- Adopting a human-centric approach for digital technologies, including artificial intelligence.
- Upskilling and re-skilling European workers, particularly digital skills.
- Modern, resource-efficient, and sustainable industries and transition to a circular economy.
- A globally competitive and world-leading industry, speeding up investment in research and innovation.

These are just some examples that demonstrate the strong links between the industrial transition and other societal developments.

Think about what this means for those working in marketing. AI has been discussed in this book. You can see it everywhere in marketing, from use in websites and chat boxes to providing and delivering a service or product.

## Chapter 3

The tasks in this chapter invite individuals to apply management and leadership knowledge and skills to choose where to open another vegetarian shop and café. The project brief follows.

## Task 3.1 Launching the new shop and café

Using the vegetarian project management case study earlier as an example, think about what needs to be done for the launch. How are you going to project-manage the launch of the opening of the new shop and café?

### Task 3.1 Responses

These should include an awareness of the difference between organising the launch of the new shop and café and then the subsequent promotion of it.

**Launch.** An appropriate response would show appreciation of the legislation required before the start-up of the premises and therefore the launch of the new business. This would depend on the location of the new shop and café. Responses should include acknowledgement of local government legislation for permission for the shop and café, and as it's food, there will be an understanding of the need to adhere to national/local food standard legislation and health and safety legislation/licensing of premises to sell food, and if alcohol is provided, this would be a separate licence. Opening times would also need to be approved by local government. It would be expected that these approvals would be in place before the physical planning of the event.

**Budget.** A realistic amount of money (as per location of the shop and café) should be noted and what it is to be spent on. The number of people who can safely be in the shop and café at any one time would also dictate how big the launch is. Promotion should match this. For example, if the promotion is related to a local celebrity opening the new shop and café, are invitations to local businesspeople by invitation only? It would not be appropriate to advertise in digital sources for a small launch, as hundreds of people turning up would not be practical. The responses need to be proportionate and show the importance of control and planning to purpose, that is, who is opening the store and how many people are invited. For example, if the shop can accommodate 20 people at once but the café can cope with 60, how could this be managed? The practical nature of the task is important here. The promotion of the event will need careful marketing. The launch could be 'soft' and quiet and be as simple as poster in the window saying we are opening on a set day – this may be the best option if the new shop and café is located in a busy area.

Alternatively, a planned event would need to consider the factors noted here, and the promotion needs to match.

The important thing to note in the responses is careful management and control throughout. Decisions would need to reflect how the event is to be organised. For example: What time is the launch? For how long, and for how many? What will be the nature of the hospitality offered? What promotions will be offered? Responses should include a logical strategy.

Not as simple a task as it may appear, but serious errors in planning could detract customers before the new venue has a chance to succeed.

Responses could note the follow-up promotional activities that would again be in proportionate and within budget.

## Chapter 4

### Task 4.1

As you're reading this book, we presume you'd like a job in 'marketing'. But doing what? Take ten minutes to note down the answer to the following: What would your dream job entail? What type of organisation would you like to work for? Or would you set up your own business, and if so, doing what?

It's important to think about and plan for your career. It may be that you don't quite know what to do specifically but that you like marketing. If this is the case, it is likely that you will embark your career in a generalist role, such as a marketing officer or assistant – this would give you a great taste of the different things to come. Join professional bodies and participate in the different networking events, where you can learn more about the different types of jobs and the vast array of industries where marketing is evident. Try to gain experience through a placement or internship, or simply volunteering. Read the latest industry magazines. The more you learn about the subject and then practice it, the quicker you will find your dream job!

## Task 4.2

Make two lists (1) of science-related marketing roles and (2) of art-related roles.

It is likely that your list will include examples around research and the collection of data, the use of data, coding and digital marketing for science-related roles, and the likes of design, content, advertising, creative campaigns, etc. for the art-related roles. If only it were that easier! There is a need for the two to work together – there is no point, for instance, in having a creative campaign if it has not been constructed in response to data about the target market and delivered by a thorough, data-informed media plan. When you review the job advertisement for any role, really investigate what type of organisation it is and how they practice marketing.

## Task 4.3

Read the Greggs case study. Where do you think marketing is evident? What type of tasks were undertaken by the team?

The Greggs Marketing Challenge is a brilliant example of university students getting first-hand experience, almost like working as a marketing consultant. The University of Sunderland won the Challenge in 2023 – well done to Mrs Kris Woods Craig Southern, Okikiola Akingbo, Olubukola Owolabi, and Connor Moore! So what aspects of marketing were considered? It is likely that you included some of the following:

- Retail, brand, product, itch, products, customers, communities, new product development, target market, consumer behaviour, product development strategy
- Growth, heritage, adaptation, experience, trial, strategic, tactical, planning, pricing
- Place, promotion, social media, influencers, multimedia, transformation, ethics
- Teamwork, presentation, brief, diversity, inclusion, competition, research

You may have even found more!

## Chapter 5

### Task 5.1 Vegetarian shop and café – costing the launch

Look back to the project management for the launch of the new vegetarian shop and café (Chapter 3). In the project management task in Chapter 3, you were invited to consider the budget and how you would allocate funds to each part of the planned launch.

For this task, go back to the budget and refine the spending and work out the calculations in detail. Start with how much you allocated in the planning of the launch and present the details in a formal report format.

### Suggested responses

The amount from the budget allocated should be practical and aligned with the planning of the launch. For example, the report would contain the following information:

Date, time, duration, number of people invited, refreshments, and whether a local celebrity is opening the shop, or if it is a quieter event. Depending on which is chosen, the marketing of the event should be appropriate – if it is an invitation-only event, are the invites going out by email, or will small poster be printed for the window?

Marketing: formal or informal?

If a formal event, the imaginary head office would be involved, and there could be a formal standard that is used (in the fictitious example). The budget should still be clear and detailed.

Costs would be operational – in the operational budget, but awareness of heating, lighting, computers. Plus, staff have time to print vouchers for a percentage off items from the shop as a welcome invitation to the new shop and café.

For the launch itself: staff costs (detail of how many hosting the event), new shop manager, their assistant, and four assistants. Manager costs per hour: £20.00 × 2 × 5 = £200.00 + 4 assistants at £10.00 × 4 × 5 = £200.00.

Catering: the food and beverages have already been bought in bulk for opening of the new shop and café.

The details of the cost breakdown would include catering per person – for example, is the newly appointed café manager going to offer food and beverages from the café range/head office or buy in? As it is a vegetarian shop, prices of fresh fruit and vegetables vary per season. Responses could suggest a light buffet at £10 per person, invitation only, so if the shop and café combined can accommodate 40 people (with room for the staff), this would be £400. Adding a sum for contingencies: £200 for a planned soft-launch budget could be as low as £1,000 figures, or could be scaled up accordingly, providing the necessary reason for the extra spending is accounted for.

## Task 5.2

Read through the jobs and quotes from participants and identify the different skills required.

Responses here could note the different skills required. For every job, there will be a list of skills. These can be generic or specific, depending on the type of role. Chapter 5 has provided extensive lists of skills; however, you will find more as you search for a job. Think about how you might gain these skills. You could gain them as part of your degree or professional body award, and perhaps you can enhance the necessary skills through work experience.

## Task 5.3

Read through the chapter and look at other job roles. What key areas of marketing knowledge are required?

Response: It is expected that those working in marketing should know what marketing is and the differing perspectives. They should know how to do various activities and the roles marketing may take (see Chapter 1 for more details).

## Chapter 6: Professional identity in marketing

### Task 6.1 Control of communications during planning for new shop

**The vegetarian store and café: control of communications:** For this task, think about the role you would undertake in terms of the control of communications during the planning for the new store. Think about who does what, when, and how.

**Responses could include:** A 'reverse engineering approach', that is, starting at the end (the opening of the new shop) from a manager's perspective. This would be ensuring what happens when and who does what/where/how. A basic project management plan is needed. A simple Excel spreadsheet could be used, with scheduled updates to make sure everything is going according to plan. The control of communications does not have to be complicated, but the manager does need to know what is happening on a daily basis and make changes if required.

## Chapter 7: Self-management

### Task 7.1

What are your best qualities? Write down as many as possible. For example: flexible, articulate, loyal, consistent, thoughtful, accurate, and so on.

Once you have your list, put the skills and qualities under headings, such as 'people skills', 'technical knowledge', and 'research skills'.

### Task 7.2

Then when you have your own list, put them in order of priority. To do this, think about how you could develop your own personal profile. A personal profile is a simple summary of who and where you are now.

Responses here would be highly individualised, but it would be expected that they include positive management and leadership skills, such as trust, ability to demonstrate excellent people and communication skills, tenacity, and creativity – the order of priority would differ in terms of the type of role/career the individual is hoping to enter, but it must be aligned. For example, creativity may come high up in the list for a marketing role, but not quite as high as organisation and planning required in a management or leadership in a marketing role. Individual responses would show an understanding and application of attributes and competencies that are role-specific.

### Task 7.3

Here is a basic job advert. How can you develop it to attract the right candidate for the new shop?

#### Fictitious job advertisement

Vegetarian shop and café manager

The vegetarian shop and café chain is expanding, and we have an exciting opportunity for a manager for a new shop opening very soon. We are looking for an enthusiastic candidate, ideally with some store and/or café management experience. This is not essential, however, as training will be given. You will have skills in food and drink preparation and food safety, with supporting qualifications. You will have excellent communication skills and, in addition, experience of working with vendors and suppliers. Working in a rota system is a requirement of the role, as once in the post, you would need to recruit an assistant shop manager and other staff to work alongside with you. The vegetarian shop and café chain offers excellent benefits, training and a career development scheme, a competitive salary of XXXXX (this would be appropriate to the region for similar roles at that time), generous holiday entitlement, and a pension scheme. If you feel this is the role for you, please apply to the online email address (stated here) by xx month/year.

After considering the qualities of the 'ideal manager', how could you develop the advert to attract the candidate you are looking for? What else do you think could be important to attract the best person for the role? To answer these questions, you may choose to consider a checklist of essential and desirable criteria, then you could give a weighting to each criterion of what you think are essential versus desirable knowledge and skills. This list will assist you in creating questions when you interview potential candidates.

## Responses to task 7.3

The advert could be improved by inserting words to create an invitation, for example: a friendlier and more personal approach with invitations such as, 'Do come and join us on this exciting new project/journey . . .' Followed up by an invitation for an informal chat about the role, with phrases such as, 'We would love to discuss this fantastic career opportunity with you! Please contact me [first name of the contact] on telephone number xxx for a chat.'

To be able to choose the right candidate, it would be necessary to draw up a list of essential and desirable criteria, as this list would help create interview questions. For example, while knowledge of merchandising, particularly in a similar shop and café or the hospitality industry, is ideal, it would be important that the new manager is friendly, adaptable, and flexible and wants to succeed. The ideal candidate would have the knowledge, skills, and experience that are shown to be needed in the response, but the chosen candidate must also be able to demonstrate enthusiasm to make a success of the new venture.

## Chapter 8

### Task 8.1 Managing a marketing campaign: the new vegetarian shop and café

How would you design and promote a marketing campaign?

Responses to the task would be a detailed understanding of the target market.

**Promotion.** Once the shop and café are operational, the marketing of it would need to within budget and planned. Responses will include an awareness of all aspects of the coordinated aspects of marketing a brand/product. This would include the marketing and promotional theories of product placement, positioning, and segmentation and targeting – the type of produce for sale and the food and beverages available for purchase in the café. Are they linked in any way to allow for a promotion? For example, if a certain vegetable is sold and a specific quantity purchased, would the purchaser also be offered a voucher for discount off a product for sale in the adjacent café? There would be an understanding of the different parts of promotion of the new shop, which mediums to market in, such as advertising and promotion in local media and on the web page of the head office. There could be an advert placed in local trade magazines and, of course, the proposed vegetable warehouses.

As there is a head office in this imaginary case study, responses would be coordinated. For example, data on prices/future stocks of fruit and vegetables for the shop will already be available from the fictitious head office of vegetarian shop and café's marketing plan.

## Chapter 9: Being a leader and a personal reflector in marketing

The tasks in this chapter invited you to explore your feelings about what a good leader means to you.

### Task 9.1

Think of a leader you admire. What personal qualities do they have? Make a note of them.

Responses could include someone from history, for example, J. F. Kennedy. Historians state he was charismatic, glamourous, an excellent communicator and public speaker, and demonstrated valued leadership qualities. Whilst he had flaws, these were not brought to the fore at that time because of his leadership at a time of great change.

### Task 9.2

Review the list you have written, then referring to Finkelstein et al.'s (2007) list of characteristics across the five areas, try to put examples against them.

### Example of possible responses

1. Positive – ability to enable transformation.

Kennedy helped prevent a war.

2. Negative – ability to deal with negative situations (people and context).

He was able to navigate through difficult situations in world tensions at that time and respond appropriately to civil tensions.

3. Conceptual – master systems.

Kennedy understood government systems and departments and how they related/interacted with each other.

4. Creative – 'think outside the box'.

He demonstrated creativity in his solution focus and by employing highly intelligent young staff and experienced and highly capable government ministers.

5. Relational – relate and build trust.

Records of people who worked with/for him state he was trustworthy and reliable, and he also demonstrated trust in his ability to negotiate with other world leaders.

## Task 9.3

Reflect back on the knowledge and skills you wrote in the tasks in the previous chapters. What have you learned about yourself, and what do you intend to work on to be a good leader in marketing?

In this task, responses would include the positive traits of leadership and how this can be demonstrated. For example, the list could include knowledge and skills in the marketing sector as appropriate, being trustworthy, possessing excellent communication skills with supporting examples, proven experience in management and leadership, and evidence of good people skills – for example, being able to demonstrate this by good examples of successful promotions of products, gained through teamworking. Very importantly, responses should show an understanding of the critical importance of consistency. In any aspect of good business practice, this can be translated to show the ability to maintain and promote a quality product or service and maintain this high standard.

**FIGURE 10.30** Students running at the beach.

## SUMMARY OF THE CHAPTER

In this chapter, we drew together the different aspects of definitions and theories of marketing and strategic management that have been discussed in the book. The fast-changing nature of marketing within advancements in technology was explored. A review of how the chapter case studies offer illustrations of what it is like to work in marketing was presented. The future of marketing within environmentalism was also examined. The possible responses to the tasks were provided in this chapter. The concluding chapter, therefore, has presented an opportunity for the application of understanding and reflection and offers guidance to individuals considering career options in marketing in different industries.

## REFERENCES

CIM. (2020) *Code of Conduct*. Available from: Governance – Royal Charter | About us | CIM (Accessed 29 April 2023).

Denlinger, K. and Seidenschwarz, C. (2023) Brands answer economic instability with marketing investments. What are the top priorities of client marketing officers in navigating economic downturns? *Deloitte Insights*, 24 January 2023. Available from: 2023 Global Marketing Trends | Deloitte Insights (Accessed 29 April 2023).

Europa, Industry 5.0. Available from: (europa.eu) (Accessed 1 May 2023).

G7 Summit. (2023) Available from: [Official] G7 Hiroshima Summit 2023 (Accessed 29 April 2023).

Global Environment Facility. (2023) Available from: What We Do | GEF (thegef.org) (Accessed 29 April 2023).

Greenpeace. (2023) Available from: Greenpeace UK (Accessed 29 April 2023).

Hunt, S.D. (2018) Advancing marketing strategy in the marketing discipline and beyond: From promise, to neglect, to prominence, to fragment (to promise?). *Journal of Marketing Management*, 34(1–2), 16–51. https://doi.org/10.1080/0267257X.2017.1326973.

Knight, P. and Yorke, M. (2003) *Assessment, Learning and Employability*. Buckingham: SRHE and Open University Press.

Kotler, P.T. and Armstrong, G. (2020) *Principles of Marketing*. 18th Edition. Harlow: Pearson.

Marr, B. (2022) Artificial intelligence and the future of marketing. *Contributor to Forbes*. Available from: Artificial Intelligence and the Future of Marketing (forbes.com) (Accessed 29 April 2023).

Percy, L. (2023) *Strategic Integrated Marketing Communications*. 4th Edition. Abingdon: Routledge.

Quesenberry, K.A. and Coolsen, M.K. (2023) *Brand Storytelling. IMC for a Digital Landscape*. London: Rowman and Littlefield.

Tóth, Z., Caruana, R., Gruber, T. and Loebbecke, C. (2022) The dawn of the AI robots: Towards a new framework of AI accountability. *Journal of Business Ethics*, 178, 895–916. https://doi.org/10.1007/s10551-022-05050-z.

Unearthed. (2023) Unearthed is Greenpeace UK's award-winning journalism project – Unearthed (Accessed 29 April 2023).

Vallance, C. (2022) *A New Chatbot Has Passed One Million Viewers in Less Than One Week*. Available from: ChatGPT: New AI chatbot has everyone talking to it – BBC News.

Watson, D. (2023) *Informal Interim Report on Business Needs Post-covid*. University of Sunderland. Unpublished.

Watson, D. and Barkas, L.A. (2018) Building a business clinic in higher education: Opportunities and challenges for students' skills development. *Journal of International Business Education*, 13, 237–248. ISSN 1649–4946.

Wilkie, W.L. and Moore, E.S. (2003) Scholarly research in marketing: Exploring the '4 eras.' *Journal of Public Policy & Marketing*, 22(2), 116–146.

## RECOMMENDED FURTHER READING

Quesenberry, K.A. and Coolsen, M.K. (2023) *Brand Storytelling. IMC for a Digital Landscape*. London: Rowman and Littlefield.

*Authors' comments This book gives an accessible insight into the opportunities and challenges of digital storytelling.*

Tóth, Z., Caruana, R., Gruber, T. and Loebbecke, C. (2022) The dawn of the AI robots: Towards a new framework of AI accountability. *Journal of Business Ethics*, 178, 895–916. https://doi.org/10.1007/s10551-022-05050-z.

*Authors' comments the authors of this article discuss critical aspects of using AI – very important to contextualise the ethics of responsible marketing.*

# Index

Note: Page numbers in *italics* indicate a figure and page numbers in **bold** indicate a table on the corresponding page.